HEREAFTER

TERRY JAMES
JONATHAN C. BRENTNER

HEREAFTER

—— IT'S FAR BETTER THAN ——
YOU CAN IMAGINE

DEFENDER

CRANE, MO

Hereafter: It's Far Better Than You Can Imagine
by Terry James and Jonathan C. Brentner

Defender Publishing
Crane, MO 65633

ISBN: 978-1-948014-74-8

Printed in the United States of America.

A CIP catalog record of this book is available from the Library of
Congress.

Cover designer: Jeffrey Mardis
Interior designer: Pamela McGrew

DEDICATION

From Terry: To dear Gail Blackburn, whose love for our Lord shone so brightly and for whom I long to see in that glorious, heavenly effulgence when Christ calls us to Himself.

From Jonathan: To my wonderful wife, Ruth: for her amazing kindness, loving support, and encouragement, without which this book would not have been possible.

To Sarah Waul, who went home to be with Jesus at age eighteen while we were writing this book. As a young girl, she came with her parents to the Bible study in our home, and was always quick to request the song, "My Lighthouse." Her unwavering reliance on the Lord for strength during her lengthy battle with cancer inspired many people. She already has a head start at enjoying many of the blessings we look forward to in the hereafter.

To my friend Todd Martin, whose hope of Heaven helped sustain him during his recent serious bout with cancer.

ACKNOWLEDGMENTS

Terry James

First and foremost, my utmost love and devotion to the Lord Jesus Christ, for whom and through whom we strive to carry out God's Great Commission of witnessing to those the Holy Spirit calls to salvation.

To my Christian brother Jonathan Brentner, who has written the greater portion of this volume, my thanks and admiration.

To my wife Margaret; Terry, Jr.; Nathan; Kerry; Dana; Jeanie; and all grandchildren, love and thanks for being there in family closeness at all times.

My very special love and thanks to daughter-close editor Angie Peters for, like in her work on our many books, shaping *Hereafter* into a volume we prayerfully hope will touch readers with Christ's soul-saving love.

Thanks, too, to all at Defender Publishing and SkyWatch TV, who have become family-close in our relationship over the years.

And to you, the reader, my prayers and hope that you be blessed mightily by the Lord as you traverse these pages.

Jonathan C. Brentner

To Terry James, my brother in the Lord and dear friend, for his concept of this book, encouragement, and guidance and support along the way.

Angie Peters for her hard work in editing this book.

J. D. Farag for opening my eyes many several years ago to all the ways the Lord was fulfilling prophecy in our world.

Jan Markell for her wonderful ministry that introduced me to so many brilliant teachers of biblical prophecy.

CONTENTS

FOREWORD

Dr. Nathan E. Jones

Having been reminded by the bathroom mirror that I was long overdue for a haircut, I found myself on a fine Saturday morning nestled comfortably into a lift seat at my favorite barbershop. This wasn't your modern-day styling salon, no; here you breathed in the scented mixture of Barbicide, pomade, shaving cream, and beard oil with just a whiff of testosterone. This old-fashioned barbershop was a "man's man'" establishment where "manly" men with their "man-cub" sons came to be expertly "manscaped" by the hefty proprietor and his crew of tonsorial artists. Tall tales, raucous joking, and staccato laughs ran up and down the line of chairs and out into the on-deck room, punctuated by the snip-snip and buzz-buzz of scissors and clippers.

As the cutting cape billowed down around my shoulders and was fastened behind my neck, it became apparent to me that something about my particular barber was amiss within this fraternal scene. The hands, though calloused and sleeved in tattoos, were slight and thin. A peek at the wall of mirrors before me revealed only that the individual standing behind me was short enough that their spiked, butch-cut, mouse-brown hair stood above my mop. A few rough pumps of the chair's lift lever

lowered me about half a foot, and I finally beheld a rather boy-like fig-
ure. It wasn't until the voice uttered, "So, whatta you have?" did it finally
dawn on me. My barber was a she!

Not that I have any problem whatsoever with a woman cutting my
hair, for I grew up with a mother and a cereal bowl; it was just that she
seemed a bit out of place. So, with my interest piqued, I conveyed my
cut preferences and then struck up a friendly interrogation. As slivers of
my hair began raining down all around me, I asked, "So, how long have
you worked here?"

"Just a few days, eh?"

"Did you come from a beauty salon?"

"No, always barbershops?"

"Does what some of these fellows say get on your nerves?"

"No, you're just one of the guys?" Oo-kay.

It wasn't until she distractedly asked me, "What do you do for a
living?" did I hesitate to respond. Now pretty sure I knew what her per-
suasion was, I softly eked out, "Um, I, uh, work in Christian ministry."

In response, her body tensed up, the clippers abruptly shut off, and
she hung there for a heartbeat unmoving. Now giving our conversation
her full attention, she spun me around, looked directly into my face, and
pressed: "So, do you think I will be going to Heaven? After all, I hear
God's not too keen on people like me." She then spun me swiftly back
around again and the clipping resumed, though at a more frantic pace.

The Lord had clearly dropped into my lap a witnessing opportunity.
Masking my quick prayer for help with a deep breath, I started, "Well,
let me ask you this, do you think you are a good person?"

"Why, yes," she replied, "I'm sure when I die and stand at the Pearly
Gates, God will let me in."

Good, I thought, *she at least believes that there is a Heaven*. So I con-
tinued, "Well, let's run a little test to see if you are indeed good enough
based on if God used only the Ten Commandments to judge one's wor-

thiness. Have you ever lied…stolen something…looked lustfully as to commit adultery in your heart?"

She responded to each with a reluctant, "Well, of course."

And, now the tipping point. "So, according to you, you are a lying, thieving, adulteress, and that's just three of the Ten Commandments. So, in God's eyes, are you good enough to be worthy of Heaven?"

Realizing she wasn't deserving based on her own merits, as the questioning intended, she began sputtering excuses as to why she will convince God she must be let in. For those reasons, it became apparent that she didn't particularly understand Heaven as the Bible describes it. "It's a magical place where you get to eat all that you want," she said. "You never work…God gives you all of the desires of your heart…and He's okay with whomever you love." Her rendition sounded like the sensual paradise so favored by Muslims.

This became yet another wonderful, God-given opportunity to share what the biblical Heaven is like. So, after a quick check to make sure the back of my head didn't have something questionable etched into it by then, I launched into a long description of the glories of the hereafter.

Then something strange happened while I was detailing the joys and wonders of eternal life in the majestic New Jerusalem on a perfected New Earth. My barber and I, at the same time, realized the room had become dead silent. Everyone there had been drawn into listening to our conversation. Even the sound of the clippers was muted, as if they were taking note as well.

To my dismay, the attention embarrassed her, and her defensive walls braced back up, deflecting anything more I had to say on the subject. And it wasn't just her; the room began to clear out as if a gas leak had been detected. Those waiting for their cuts suddenly realized they had other places to be. Those already seated became fine with their haircuts as they were and became eager to pay. And, when the stampede out of the shop had finally died down, the trapped barbers congregated in front of a widescreen TV, seeming to stare through the ballgame rather than watch it. My cut completed, I was summarily dismissed. I paid the bill and hovered around for a bit hoping for any follow-up discussion. However, receiving no bites, I left, deflated.

To this day, that remains the oddest witnessing experience of my life. It took many weeks of searching the Scripture before I came to two realizations. First, whereas the Bible assures us that something infinitely better awaits us in our future if we surrender our lives to Jesus Christ, there's a price to be paid *after* receiving it. Most folks aren't willing to give up their earthly sinful pleasures to "walk as children of light" (Ephesians 5:8). And second, the majority of people grossly underestimate the sheer awesomeness of Heaven as well as the absolute terror of Hell. The result is they so greatly fear life after death that they cast all thoughts of it from their minds and hope that such recollections will never intrude upon their consciousnesses again.

How tragic! Misunderstanding our eternal destiny this side of death robs us of our only opportunity to embrace our loving Savior's forgiveness and salvation. We also lose the jubilant hope Christ provides when it comes to expecting the glories He longs to share with His children. The delights and wonders of Heaven make the paltry pleasures of this current world appear as if they were nothing. However, most people live out their lives pining for such deprivations, so they miss out.

Heaven forbid that Christians also find themselves in such a state! That's why I am so thankful that trusted Christian teachers such as Terry and Jonathan have set out to produce a book that corrects our misunderstandings concerning what the Bible teaches about the hereafter. The biblical truths about our glorious future they will impart will establish you on a firm foundation regarding eternity and will fortify you against the sorrows of this temporal life. The Lord will use this knowledge to comfort your soul when the fierce storms of fallen, earthly living rob you of your aspirations and dreams, refocusing you instead on the grand adventures that lie ahead.

I pray this book will make its way into the hands of that lost barber and, someday soon, together we will experience glorious life everlasting. I'll see you there!

~DR. NATHAN E. JONES
Lamb & Lion Ministries
March 2023

THE PROMISE OF PROPHECY

The best we can hope for in this life is a knothole peek at the shining realities ahead. Yet a glimpse is enough. It's enough to convince our hearts that whatever sufferings and sorrows currently assail us aren't worthy of comparison to that which waits over the horizon.

~JONI EARECKSON TADA, Christian author and founder of
Joni and Friends

W orld War II British Prime Minister Winston Churchill addressed his nation's war-weary people at a time when everything looked foreboding and bleak. They had long endured Adolf Hitler's bombardment of their cities. London was in shambles as a result. And then the assault stopped as Hitler took his rage and intention to enslave people in a different direction.

Mr. Churchill, in his authoritative British voice and with inimitable and typical bulldog resolve, told the people during this speech: "Now this is not the end. It is not even the beginning of the end. But it is, perhaps, the end of the beginning."

They had taken the brunt of the Nazi assault and survived. Now they would wage the war in a way that would bring victory to Britain.

This, of course, is exactly how it happened five years later. The Allies experienced victory, but with the greatest carnage left in the war's wake ever before experienced.

Even though it's spiritual warfare, believers in Jesus Christ—especially those who view Bible prophecy from the premillennial, pre-Tribulation perspective—can get a sense of those engendered by that war of the last century. Today we look around the national and geopolitical landscape and sense an assault from the chief progenitor of all hatred and war, the Devil himself. Every day we feel the continual barrage of cultural and societal attacks that come from anti-God minions who exhibit the end-times characteristics the Apostle Paul explained in Romans 1:28–32:

> And even as they did not like to retain God in their knowledge, God gave them over to a reprobate mind, to do those things which are not convenient; Being filled with all unrighteousness, fornication, wickedness, covetousness, maliciousness; full of envy, murder, debate, deceit, malignity; whisperers, backbiters, haters of God, despiteful, proud, boasters, inventors of evil things, disobedient to parents, Without understanding, covenant breakers, without natural affection, implacable, unmerciful: Who knowing the judgment of God, that they which commit such things are worthy of death, not only do the same, but have pleasure in them that do them.

When Churchill and the British people finally emerged from their bunkers after enduring the wrath of the Nazi bombers, they saw only devastation. They had nothing to look forward to but a life-and-death struggle with the one they viewed as the Devil incarnate—Adolf Hitler. The world immediately surrounding them offered only days, weeks, months, and years of hardship, sweat, blood, and tears as they looked toward rebuilding their homeland.

This is where the bleakness of their perspective on the future differs stupendously from ours. In spite of Satan's continual war against humanity, as believers in Christ, we live in the hope of a glorious eternity.

At this moment, those who follow Christ as well as unbelievers face a world worse than that faced by the people of Hitler's day. Rumors of war portend a devastation far in excess of the recent ravages suffered by the Ukrainian people under Russian assault. This battle has the potential to explode into a nuclear catastrophe.

There can be no rebuilding by human construction if all-out nuclear warfare devastates the planet. Earth would, should such a thing eventuate, become uninhabitable for centuries, if the physical laws governing the half-life of nuclear radiation were to play out.

Jesus, the Creator of all that is, warned that there is coming a time in human history worse than ever experienced. Matthew 24:21 records His words about this:

> For then shall be great tribulation, such as was not since the beginning of the world to this time, no, nor ever shall be.

However, in Revelation 3:10–11a, Jesus promised to keep all those who believe in Him out of this most horrendous time of history yet to play out; He will come for us before the judgments of that day begin:

> Because thou hast kept the word of my patience, I also will keep thee from the hour of temptation, which shall come upon all the world, to try them that dwell upon the earth. Behold, I come quickly.

The Apostle John, who recorded these words, remembered when the Lord had made a similar pledge to His disciples in the Upper Room after telling them He was going to leave. Here is what He said to the representatives of all those who would put their faith in the Savior during the current Age of Grace:

Let not your heart be troubled: ye believe in God, believe also in me. In my Father's house are many mansions: if it were not so, I would have told you. I go to prepare a place for you. And if I go and prepare a place for you, I will come again, and receive you unto myself; that where I am, there ye may be also. (John 14:1–3)

The future apostles understood almost nothing of the true meaning of His words at the time; it was a mystery. They asked Him where He was going, as a matter of fact. Jesus was, of course, speaking of His upcoming death, burial, and resurrection, followed by His ascension into Heaven.

In his letters to the Corinthian believers, the Apostle Paul would later explain this mystery about Christ coming for them and all who believe:

Behold, I shew you a mystery; We shall not all sleep, but we shall all be changed, in a moment, in the twinkling of an eye, at the last trump: for the trumpet shall sound, and the dead shall be raised incorruptible, and we shall be changed. For this corruptible must put on incorruption, and this mortal must put on immortality. So when this corruptible shall have put on incorruption, and this mortal shall have put on immortality, then shall be brought to pass the saying that is written, Death is swallowed up in victory. O death, where is thy sting? O grave, where is thy victory? The sting of death is sin; and the strength of sin is the law. But thanks be to God, which giveth us the victory through our Lord Jesus Christ. Therefore, my beloved brethren, be ye stedfast, unmovable, always abounding in the work of the Lord, forasmuch as ye know that your labour is not in vain in the Lord. (1 Corinthians 15:51–58)

Suffice to say that Paul's words, inspired by the Holy Spirit, should be a powerful stimulant for all believers while we look forward to Christ's any-moment call to us in the Rapture. The words of Scripture will be our basis for exploring the wonders that await us in eternity.

We as God's children living in this Age of Grace are on the verge of experiencing what, like Winston Churchill said in World War II, is "the end of the beginning." We are at the end of the beginning of the wrap-up of the turbulent Church Age. Jesus will soon snatch believers from this fallen planet and our exciting journey into eternal bliss will begin.

HEAVEN'S HOMECOMING HIGHLIGHTS

These authors are most blessed to have been prompted by the Holy Spirit to set upon this book project, which we gave the title *Hereafter*. Its subtitle, *It's Far Better Than You Can Even Imagine*, encompasses the great expectation for all believers in the Lord Jesus Christ. Considering the lateness of the hour, prophetically speaking, we believe it's an exciting and highly appropriate volume for New Testament saints—especially for those who view Bible prophecy from the pre-Tribulation, premillennial perspective.

The title came upon remembering the late, great broadcaster Paul Harvey's words regarding a dental product he promoted: "If you want to keep your pearly whites from here to hereafter, you need [whatever that product was]."

Paul Harvey professed to be a believer in Christ. Thus, by "hereafter," we presume he was referring to that magnificent sphere to which believers ascend instantaneously when we finish our work/journey in this foreign land we call "earth."

"Hereafter," therefore, is the one topic that should draw our attention. This life is but a vapor, as Scripture says. Eternity is, well, *forever*. Heaven is our real home.

With this in mind, we invite you to think about your eternal home. We strongly believe most of the currently living New Testament saints will experience the Rapture of the Church before they die. Jesus could transport us into the eternal realm at any moment—what a thrilling prospect to consider!

Sadly, many pastors in churches today don't dwell to any extent upon our wondrous expectation. Most refuse to talk about the Rapture and rarely say the words "eternal life," even when explaining the Gospel.

THIS RAPTURE GENERATION

Some might regard the above heading as audacious. "This Rapture Generation" implies that people alive now are those who will, without doubt, be the generation of believers who go to Christ in the Rapture, doesn't it?

Those who have named specific dates for this stupendous event have earned consternation through the years, and deservedly so. Jesus declared that no one but the Father knows the day or hour when it will occur. And certainly, to date, that truth has played out exactly as He said it would.

Yet, at the same time, the Apostle Paul implied that he himself might be alive at the time of the Rapture (1 Corinthians 15:51; 1 Thessalonians 4:17). Such was the expectation in the early days of the Church: Jesus, the early Christ-followers believed, might appear at any time to catch His Bride up to Heaven. Yet Paul has been dead for almost two thousand years, and the Rapture remains a future event.

Does that mean God's Word (the "Word" who, in fact, is the Lord Jesus Christ, according to John 1:1) is less than truthful? We know the answer to that is a resounding, "No." God cannot lie; therefore, we are to think through Paul's words with our Holy Spirit-given discernment to understand the daring statement. Paul's declaration was as audacious as our subhead above, we think.

So, what is this seeming contradiction all about?

The answer, we believe, is found in another familiar statement by Paul, one we use frequently in studying the Rapture:

> Looking for that blessed hope, and the glorious appearing of the great God and our Saviour Jesus Christ. (Titus 2:13)

We believe that wrapped up in this profound statement of faith is an instruction to all believers. During this Age of Grace (Church Age), we're always to be earnestly expecting Jesus to snatch us from this fallen sphere at any moment. This instruction has been in effect since the Church was born (see Acts chapter 2). Believers during the times of the New Testament and early Church history regarded Jesus' appearing, the Rapture, as something that could take place in their lifetimes. With the resurgence of teaching on this matter, many saints today live with the same anticipation. As a matter of fact, all who love the prospect of Christ's appearing are promised a crown of righteousness (see chapter 6). With this in mind, the title, "This Rapture Generation," is appropriate for those of us who are believers now. Jesus will come for us in the Rapture at any moment—perhaps today!

We hope to go much deeper in expressing this certainty. Our goal is to go farther into this matter with each and every chapter.

The Lord is brilliantly illuminating the signals of His appearing for those with discerning spirits. He's unfolding prophetic signs of such unmistakable importance that we would have to look in another direction to miss just how near we are to the Tribulation. The Rapture is thus right at the exit door of human history for believers in Jesus Christ.

Unfortunately, most who should be helping God's children focus on the lateness of the hour continue to feed only baby food about how to grow into Christian adulthood. The focus of "your best life now" teachings leave folks woefully unprepared for what's coming.

Such spiritual food isn't bad, of course; it's necessary for spiritual growth. However, the lateness of the hour requires us to take a hard look at God's prophetic timeline. We are very near the instant of Rapture. *This is almost certainly the Rapture generation, and we cannot feel sheepish in declaring it.*

Tell everyone you know, using your own words, the soul-saving truth encompassed by Paul's Holy Spirit-given formula for going in the Rapture when Christ calls:

> That if thou shalt confess with thy mouth the Lord Jesus, and shalt believe in thine heart that God hath raised him from the dead, thou shalt be saved. For with the heart man believeth unto righteousness; and with the mouth confession is made unto salvation. (Romans 10:9–10)

Terry's dear, personal friend, the late Dr. Dave Breese, once portrayed in his unsurpassed eloquence, the following about the hereafter:

> Let each of us be finally reminded that the story of the future is not simply that of one day after another ad infinitum. No indeed! There is a glorious future for the Church, and there is a dismal future for the world. The sojourn of the Church in this world will come to an instantaneous end, at which time every believer will be taken from this dark planet to the glory which is to come.
>
> At the moment of that transition, each of us will receive a new body, a glorified body that is not unlike the body of Christ himself. We will at this point be given the capacity to feel, to appreciate, to enjoy all of the unspeakably wonderful things

that will be ours in eternity. The Scripture says, "In thy presence is fullness of joy; at thy right hand are pleasures for evermore" (Psalm 16:11).

So great will be the delights of heaven that they are impossible to describe under the constraints, the limitations of human language. It may, therefore, be well to exercise a sanctified imagination, to ask the question, "What will it be like when Jesus comes?" The answer, of course, is that it will be like nothing we can imagine in all of life. There is no human experience that resembles in any but the palest fashion the ecstasy that will be ours when we step across the great divide into the fadeless light of heaven.

What is heaven like? The answer must be that heaven is not exactly like anything that we know in this world. We do well to take the greatest joys of earth and multiply them by a thousand times. Only then do we have even the beginning of the joys that will be ours in heaven.

The Christian is invited to use his "sanctified imagination" to think of golden streets, ivory palaces, a city where there is no night, and endless "pleasure forever more." In heaven also, we will have the opportunity to meet the saints who have gone before and, of course, loved ones who have in earlier days moved from the Church militant to the Church triumphant. How wonderful to contemplate that golden moment when the Church will be translated from this world to the world to come. What a moment that will be!

The real point is that we be prepared for that moment. The preparation is that we must be Christians. A Christian is one who believes the gospel of Jesus Christ, who has accepted the Son of the living God as personal Saviour. Because of the shed blood of Jesus Christ, the sufficient sacrifice for sin, each person in all of the world is invited to receive the free gift, the gift of God, which is everlasting life. The single requirement is faith alone. By believing in Jesus Christ—who He was and what He did for man on the cross—by that act of faith I receive the gift of God, which is life eternal.

Meanwhile, in these days, let us gather together at the cross, recognizing Jesus Christ as the Saviour whose sacrifice made eternal life possible. While laboring for Him here, let us also anticipate the sound of the trumpet when we will be caught up to be with Him.[1]

Such is the task before us as we seek to communicate the joyous adventure ahead for all New Testament saints that begins with the Rapture of the Church.

Chapter 1

FOR THE JOY

I am certain of this, fellow-Christians, that as we have been
together in the labor, duty, danger and distress, so shall we be
in the great recompense and deliverance. And as we have been
scorned and despised together, so shall we be crowned and
honored together; and we who have gone through the day of
sadness shall enjoy together that day of gladness; and those who
have been with us in persecutions and prison, shall be with us also
in that palace of consolation.

~RICHARD BAXTER, *The Saints' Everlasting Rest*[2]

What gets us through the fierce storms of life? Where do we look
for hope when painful circumstances turn our world upside
down? Isn't it the joy of eternity set before us on the pages of Scripture?
That's where we find the hope that enables us to look beyond the wickedness, lawlessness, violence, and sorrows of this current age to the over-
the-top delights of the hereafter, our wonderful adventure that begins
with Jesus' appearing to take us home to Heaven.

*It all comes back to our Savior; He's the source of all our joy both now
and forever.*

It's one thing to say an eternal outlook on life comforts hearts in the midst of affliction, but quite another to do so when painful circumstances assail us for lengthy periods of time. Both writers have felt many heartbreaks and, as a result, we know a forward look to the bliss of Heaven brings sweet relief to the soul.

We will share our stories as well as that of the remarkable Richard Baxter on the pages that follow.

JONATHAN'S WORDS: "FOR THE JOY SET BEFORE ME"

I remember a time about twenty-five years ago when I longed for an escape from all that life seemed to be. I felt both shame and despair. As I searched for hope amid the chaos and sorrow, the Lord repeatedly reminded me of these words from Hebrews 12:2:

> Looking unto Jesus the author and finisher of our faith; who for the joy that was set before him endured the cross, despising the shame, and is set down at the right hand of the throne of God.

As I considered Jesus' anguish in light of the simple words from Hebrews 12:2, "for the joy," my focus shifted away from my adversities to the delights of Heaven. My change of perspective began as I thought about the Lord's agony on the cross.

No other human being suffered as much pain and grief as Jesus. Before the crucifixion, He endured unjust trials, the mockery of soldiers, and physical suffering from the bloody crown of thorns placed on His head. It wasn't uncommon for men to die from the flogging the Romans inflicted on the condemned before crucifying them.

While He was on the cross, Jesus felt the momentary, agonizing separation from His Beloved Father as He bore all our sins upon Himself. On top of all that, He heard the scoffing and ridicule of those who condemned Him. Can you imagine how it felt to hear the insults of those He came to redeem? Today, who would even consider ridiculing people moments before they are put to death for their crimes? It seems barbaric to our current way of thinking.

The writer of Hebrews said the way Jesus endured all the anguish as well as the shame of being on the cross was by looking to the "joy" ahead for Him in glory. Perhaps He remembered the glory He once enjoyed in Heaven and looked forward to being with His Beloved Father again. Or maybe thoughts of the time when He would bring His Bride, the Church, with Him back to His Father's house helped Him withstand the agony of the torture (John 14:2–3, 17:24). In the midst of unimaginable pain, the Lord gave us an example to follow by looking forward to the bliss ahead.

These thoughts led me to write a short essay that I titled "The Land of What Will Be." In it, I contrasted the joy of forever with what I called "The Land of What Might Have Been." Exploring the contrast between my past bitter disappointments and the wonders before me in eternity enabled me to put my distressing "what might have been" thoughts behind me (see that essay in appendix A).

The phrase "for the joy" speaks volumes, doesn't it? Paul likely had Jesus' example in mind when he wrote Romans 8:18:

> For I reckon that the sufferings of this present time are not worthy to be compared with the glory which shall be revealed in us.

The apostle suffered great affliction during his efforts to spread the Gospel, but in his mind, all of his troubles paled in comparison to the wonders awaiting him in Heaven.

Regardless of where the Lord takes us, whether it's down roads of triumph or into areas where we'll face fierce opposition and even persecution, the Bible assures us that something better remains in our future: the happiness set before us in eternity.

TERRY'S WORDS:
"I WAS RACING TOWARD HEAVEN"

This is the story of what happened when I suffered a widow-maker heart attack in April of 2011. (The widow-maker occurs when there's a blockage in the artery that runs directly into the heart. If not cleared immediately, the heart stops and the person dies.)

My heart did stop—on, the hospital records show, four different times. I remember three of those times because, each time it stopped, I was instantly in front of the same huge throng of magnificent heavenly beings. They were handsome and beautiful young men and women—smiling broadly with great, energetic enthusiasm—who were bidding me to come to them. They looked no older than their middle-to-late twenties.

Each time I was with them, things started darkening from the spectacular brightness of that realm. That's when the doctors in the cath lab[3] hit me with the defibrillation paddles to restart my heart. By the third time it happened, I definitely remember not wanting to leave that joy-filled place.

That third time, I wasn't in front of the group; I was among them. We were running swiftly and effortlessly toward a destination I couldn't see at the moment. They had their hands raised and were looking over at me, laughing out of sheer delight, making me sense they were saying, "Isn't this the most wonderful thing ever?!"

It sure was, and I didn't want to leave. However, being blind, things faded to black yet again, and I was again in darkness on the table. The doctor had removed the blockage; I was back to stay.

I know the raised arms and bright smiles were the way these runners were saying as they looked over at me: "This is a race we are running together...and we're already in a victory lap!"

Many factors mark this experience as miraculous, but an important one is that the interventionist cardiologist (a doctor who specializes in such procedures), who just happened to be the top guy in our state, was presenting a lecture to physicians in a room next to the room where I was repeatedly being brought back to life. He was teaching the exact procedure that saved my life.

The medical staff called him in, and within minutes, he performed the life-saving procedure. "That's quite a coincidence," a nonbeliever might say. But with God, there is no such thing; it's all a matter of His providence.

Statistics show that around 95 percent of those who have my heart ailment don't live to recount it. However, our Lord pays no attention to such odds, thankfully!

The doctors were so impressed with my complete recovery—without major damage to my heart, etc.—that they presented me with the "Cardiology Patient of the Year" award, which now sits on a shelf in my study as a reminder of what happened.

More importantly, they invited me back to speak at their convention, where I was able to testify to God's grace and explain the salvation that's found only in the Lord Jesus Christ. The audience applauded enthusiastically when I finished, so I'm trusting the message was well received.

The bottom line is that God used this dramatic event, just as He has used my blindness, to cause me to focus on the purpose for which He brought me into this life in the first place. It's all wrapped up in the book of Hebrews. As a matter of fact, the writer of that book sums it all up rather nicely. Hebrews 12:1–8 is a magnificent statement of our Lord's intervention, out of His great love for us, in our lives. Here, then, is the story—*my* story—of how our Lord disciplines His children and keeps us in the center of His holy will:

> Wherefore seeing we also are compassed about with so great a cloud of witnesses, let us lay aside every weight, and the sin which doth so easily beset us, and let us run with patience the race that is set before us, looking unto Jesus the author and finisher of our faith; who for the joy that was set before him endured the cross, despising the shame, and is set down at the right hand of the throne of God. For consider him that endured such contradiction of sinners against himself, lest ye be wearied and faint in your minds. Ye have not yet resisted unto blood, striving against sin. And ye have forgotten the exhortation which speaketh unto you as unto children, My son, despise not thou the chastening of the Lord, nor faint when thou art rebuked of him: For whom the Lord loveth he chasteneth, and scourgeth every son whom he receiveth. If ye endure chastening, God dealeth with you as with sons; for what son is he whom the father chasteneth not but if ye be without chastisement, whereof all are partakers, then are ye bastards, and not sons.

By so intervening in our lives, God is sovereignly preparing us for the hereafter—that eternal, heavenly state wherein the Lord Jesus will reward us for our faithfulness while we served as His royal ambassadors during our physical lives.

We all want to hear Him say at that moment: "Well done, good, faithful servant. Welcome into the joy of your salvation."

RICHARD BAXTER'S STORY:
THE THRILL OF FOREVER

In his book, *Hot Tub Religion,* author and theologian J. I. Packer recounts the story of Richard Baxter, a Puritan preacher who lived during seventeenth century England. Baxter persevered in his work for the Lord despite life-long suffering and intense pain.

Packer describes Baxter's severe health issues:

He was a chronically sick Puritan, tubercular from his teens and suffering constantly from dyspepsia, kidney stones, headaches, toothaches, swollen limbs, intermittent bleeding in his extremities, and other troubles, and all before the days of painkilling drugs. Yet he was always energetic, outgoing, and uncomplaining, and utterly health-minded, even though sometimes (and who can wonder?) a trifle short-tempered.[4]

Despite all his limitations, Baxter served as the pastor of a church in a town called Kidderminster in England, wrote several books, and actively evangelized the entire city where he preached until health limitations forced him to retire at the age of forty-five.

Then, during the next thirty years, when…he was no longer able to hold a pastoral charge, he wrote so much that he now has a niche in history as the most prolific English theologian of all time.[5]

Baxter was the author of 141 books, including *The Saints' Everlasting Rest,* which many today regard as a classic. He wrote the following about his suffering in this timeless work:

Some of us are languishing under continual weakness and groaning under most grievous pains, crying in the morning, "Would God it were evening!" and in the evening, "Would God it were morning!"—weary of going, weary of sitting, weary of standing, weary of lying, weary of eating, weary of speaking, weary of walking, weary of our very friends, weary of ourselves. Oh! how often has this been mine own case![6]

How did this sickly, pain-stricken man accomplish so much in his pastoral ministry and afterward become such a prolific writer? Baxter's secret consisted of meditating on the joys ahead for him in eternity for half an hour each day. Rather than focus on his ill health, he spent that time focusing on the delights of Heaven.

Baster wrote this about his habit of daily meditating on the thrill of forever:

Sit down and think about this eternity. Study frequently, study thoroughly, this one word: eternity. And when you learned thoroughly that one word.... What! live, and never die? Rejoice, and ever rejoice![7]

The study of biblical prophecy regarding the end times has progressed much from Baxter's day. Our understanding has grown considerably as we near the time of fulfillment for many of the Bible's prophecies, especially those revealed in the book of Revelation. Yet his counsel, that of spending time each day contemplating what's ahead, still resonates at a time when the number of distractions due to the hustle and bustle of modern life has increased exponentially in just the past fifty years.

Beyond the Tyranny of the Moment

As a result of the hectic lifestyle of the twenty-first century, we all fight what pastor and author Paul David Tripp calls the "tyranny of the moment," which continually pulls our attention away from the hereafter, making it all the more difficult to focus on its many pleasures.

He wrote the following about how our current existence makes having a heavenly mindset so difficult:

> It's hard to live with eternity in view. Life does shrink to the moment again and again. There are moments when it seems that the most important thing in life is getting through this traffic, winning this argument, or satisfying this sexual desire. There are moments when our happiness and contentment shrink to getting those new shoes or the steak that is just ten minutes away. There are moments when who we are, who God is, and where this whole thing is going shrink into the background of the thoughts, emotions, and needs of the moment.[8]

His words sum up our need of daily reminders of the joy we will experience in eternity, the biblical specifics of the hereafter. A blurry or faulty image of Paradise can't compete with the allure of what we see around us each day.

If we believe the stuff of this life is superior to that of Heaven, we will resist turning our hearts toward eternity and anticipating Jesus' imminent return. The problem with such a perspective is that our temporal aspirations eventually evaporate, and disappointment floods our souls. Even when we happen to reach our hard-sought goals, a nagging since of emptiness often remains; *Is this all there is to life?*

On the other hand, where do we turn when the doctor says, "Cancer"? What happens when a spouse says, "Goodbye," or when we suffer a painful affliction with no cure in sight? Is it possible for a sense of joy to return even when we experience great loss? Yes, but it takes the mindset of Paul in 2 Corinthians 4:17–18 for such a hopeful outlook to return after hardships ravage our souls:

> For our light affliction, which is but for a moment, worketh for us a far more exceeding and eternal weight. While we look not at the things which are seen, but at the things which are not seen: for the things which are seen are temporal; but the things which are not seen are eternal.

Notice that the apostle instructs us to set our minds on things that are eternal. However, how can we do that if we don't know what the Bible says about what happens after our temporal existence disappears?

It's our prayer that the splendors of our future discussed in this book will turn your gaze heavenward, to the glory ahead for you in eternity—and that, as a result, your perspective will become increasingly similar to what the Apostle Paul expressed in 2 Corinthians 4:17–18.

Chapter 2

GLORY BOUND

The apostolic church thought more about the Second Coming of Jesus Christ than about death and heaven. The early Christians were looking, not for a cleft in the ground called a grave but for a cleavage in the sky called Glory.

~ALEXANDER MACLAREN, Christian preacher and scholar

During the early decades of the twentieth century, the song, "This Train Is Bound for Glory," became a popular gospel tune and was later recorded by talented singers such as Johnny Cash. It wasn't a coincidence that, during this time, a belief in the pre-Tribulation Rapture had already become a mainstay at many Bible-believing churches in America as well as throughout much of the world. Pastors boldly encouraged their flocks with the hope of Jesus' imminent appearing to take them home to glory *before* the onset of the seven-year Tribulation.

Unfortunately, much has changed during the past twenty-five years. The word "Rapture" has become taboo in many churches today, even in numerous houses of worship that claim to believe in the divine inspiration and inerrancy of Scripture.

Because of this intense opposition and scoffing, it's necessary to establish the Rapture's validity before further exploring the many delights we will experience when Jesus comes to take us to our ultimate destination and home: Heaven.

THE RAPTURE: A BIBLICAL EVENT

Scripture provides several details regarding the sequence of events referred to as the "Rapture." The late Dr. Ed Hindson, former professor at Liberty University, Bible scholar, and author, put it this way:

> If you disagree on the timing of the rapture, please don't tell people, "There's never going to be a rapture." No, there must be a rapture or the Bible is not true. There must be a time when the archangel shouts, when the trumpet sounds, and the dead in Christ are raised and the living are caught up (1 Thessalonians 4:13–18). We may differ on the timing of the rapture but not the fact of the rapture.[9]

The Rapture is a scripturally sound occurrence regardless of its timing in respect to the seven-year Tribulation. The events described in 1 Thessalonians 4:14–17 must take place in the future:

> For since we believe that Jesus died and rose again, even so, through Jesus, God will bring with him those who have fallen asleep. For this we declare to you by a word from the Lord, that we who are alive, who are left until the coming of the Lord, will not precede those who have fallen asleep. For the Lord himself will descend from heaven with a cry of command, with the voice of an archangel, and with the sound of the trumpet of God. And the dead in Christ will rise first. Then we who are alive, who are left, will be caught up together with them in the clouds to

meet the Lord in the air, and so we will always be with the Lord. Therefore encourage one another with these words. (ESV)

We find references to this same event in John 14:2–3; 1 Corinthians 15:50–55; Philippians 3:20–21; Romans 8:23–25; Titus 2:11–14; and Colossians 3:4. Putting these passages together, we produced the following chain of events, all of which will take place suddenly and almost simultaneously:

1. Jesus descends from Heaven (1 Thessalonians 4:16).
2. There's a "cry of command," along with the shout of the archangel (1 Thessalonians 4:16).
3. The "trumpet of God" sounds (1 Thessalonians 4:16).
4. Jesus first raises the dead in Christ with immortal bodies and joins them to the souls He brings with Him (1 Thessalonians 4:14–16; 1 Corinthians 15:52).
5. In the "twinkling of an eye," believers who are alive receive their immortal bodies and meet Jesus in the air (1 Thessalonians 4:17; 1 Corinthians 15:50-54; Philippians 3:20–21; Romans 8:23–25).
6. Jesus takes His Bride, the Church, to the place He's prepared for them in His Father's house (John 14:2–3, 17:24).
7. We appear with Jesus in glory (Colossians 3:4).

These actions represent what we today refer to as the "Rapture." It's not a fictional belief based on mysterious visions from the nineteenth century, as many claim, but an actual event described in several places within the pages of the New Testament.

We have a solid scriptural basis for our "blessed hope" (Titus 2:11–14). In Romans 8:23–24, Paul wrote about the "redemption of our bodies," then said, "For in this hope we were saved" (ESV). This isn't just any expectation, it's an anticipation of meeting Jesus in the air, which is embedded in the saving message of the Gospel.

RAPTURE'S ROOTS IN THE EARLY CHURCH

Another objection often comes from those who claim that no one in the early Church believed in a pre-Tribulation Rapture. Please don't fall for that lie; it simply isn't true. The New Testament hope of Jesus' imminent appearing spilled over into the writings of many early writers.

In AD 180, theologian and bishop Irenaeus wrote *Against Heresies* to refute the errors of Gnosticism, which posed a great threat to the Church at the time. In Book 5, Chapter 29 of the book, he wrote:

> And therefore, when in the end the Church shall be suddenly caught up from this, it is said, "There shall be Tribulation such as has not been since the beginning, neither shall be."[10]

Irenaeus used the same Greek word for "caught up," *harpazo*, that Paul used in 1 Thessalonians 4:17, and placed this event ahead of the events Jesus referred to in the context of Matthew 24:21. Irenaeus believed a time of "Tribulation" would follow the sequence of events Paul described in 1 Thessalonians 4:14–17. This respected early Church leader didn't combine the Rapture and Second Coming as many do today, but separated the events with an intervening period of God's judgment on the earth.

Cyprian, a bishop in the city of Carthage during the early third century AD, wrote the following in his book, *Treatises of Cyprian*:

> We who see that terrible things have begun, and know that still more terrible things are imminent, may regard it as the greatest advantage to depart from it as quickly as possible. Do you not

give God thanks, do you not congratulate yourself, that by an early departure you are taken away, and delivered from the shipwrecks and disasters that are imminent? Let us greet the day which assigns each of us to his own home, which snatches us hence, and sets us free from the snares of the world and restores us to paradise and the kingdom.[11]

The "early departure" of the Church from the earth before further disasters would occur is the pre-Tribulation Rapture. This reference to "snatches us hence" resembles the catching-up of the Church referred to in 1 Thessalonians 4:17. Cyprian believed Jesus would take believers out of the world to "paradise" before the Tribulation period.

Saint Ephraim of Edessa was a monk, a poet, a hymn writer, and a preacher during the fourth century AD. The following excerpt from his sermon entitled "On the Last Times, the Antichrist, and the End of the World" also places Jesus' return for His Church ahead of the entire Tribulation period:

Believe you me, dearest brother, because the coming (advent) of the Lord is nigh, believe you me, because the end of the world is at hand, believe me, because it is the very last time. Or do you not believe unless you see with your eyes? See to it that this sentence be not fulfilled among you of the prophet who declares: "Woe to those who desire to see the day of the Lord!" For all the saints and elect of God are gathered, prior to the tribulation that is to come, and are taken to the Lord lest they see the confusion that is to overwhelm the world because of our sins.[12]

These three excerpts demonstrate an early belief in Jesus taking His Church out of the world before God's judgment falls and sufficiently dispel the claim that no one in the early Church believed in the pre-Tribulation Rapture.

Yes, Cyprian and Ephraim believed Jesus was coming for His Church in their day because of what they saw happening around them. Does that mean they were wrong to have such a hope? Not at all.

As noted in the introduction, the Apostle Paul believed he might be alive at the time of Rapture as well. It's been the expectation of like-minded believers throughout much of Church history. (See appendix B for a list of twelve reasons explaining what makes today different from previous times in history in regard to Jesus' return to the earth.)

Hope in Jesus' Appearing

Now that we've established the Rapture as a biblical event with historic roots dating back to the early centuries of the Church, let's look at why it's such a precious hope for those of us who excitedly anticipate it occurring in the near future.

1. The Rapture is when we will see Jesus. In 1 Corinthians 13:12, we read Paul's words:

> For now we see in a mirror dimly, but then face to face. Now I know in part; then I shall know fully, even as I have been fully known.

The Rapture is when the Lord will clear away the fog of this life and we will see Jesus "face to face." As we walk with the Lord here below, we sometimes feel the "fog of war" similar to what those engaged in active combat experience. We have an enemy who messes with our feelings and thoughts while at the same time bringing fierce opposition to our doorstep, even from those once close to us. We long for the time when Jesus will clear away the haze so we not only see Him, but hear His welcoming voice as we take our first steps in Paradise.

When the Rapture happens, life's current hardships will pale in comparison to being with Christ in Heaven. Great Christian evangelist Billy Graham once said this about our glorious expectation:

The most thrilling thing about heaven is that Jesus Christ will be there. I will see Him face to face. Jesus Christ will meet us at the end of life's journey.

And here are the Apostle John's words about our experience at the time of Jesus' appearing:

Beloved, now are we the sons of God, and it doth not yet appear what we shall be: but we know that, when he shall appear, we shall be like him; for we shall see him as he is. (1 John 3:2)

Something about our first glimpse of the Savior will radically transform us. Although tens of millions of living saints, or many more, will be headed skyward at the same time, somehow we all will see Jesus, and He will see each of us. We can't explain how this will happen, but we know that nothing is impossible with our Lord.

2. The Rapture is when we will receive our new bodies. At the time of the Rapture, Jesus will give us incorruptible and immortal bodies (Philippians 3:20–21; 1 Corinthians 15:51–55). The saddest aspect of pastors ignoring the topic of the Rapture is in the almost total absence of teaching concerning the imperishable bodies we'll receive when Jesus comes for us. We don't recall hearing a sermon in the past twenty-five years in which a pastor talked about this especially wonderful aspect of our "blessed hope." Yet this was a foundational hope of the saints during New Testament times.

Sadly, a growing number of Bible teachers claim 1 Corinthians 15:51–55 refers to what happens at our conversion rather than our future receipt of incorruptible bodies. Such an interpretation is deeply flawed and contradicts both the context (all of 1 Corinthians 15) and the meaning of the words Paul uses to describe our resurrection bodies.

We realize that, as we experience the effects of aging, we increasingly cherish the promise of receiving renewed bodies. However, it's important to note that our future immortal bodies will even be a vast improvement over *all* earthly ones—even over those that are young, strong, and healthy.

Many young people endure illnesses and physical ailments from which they never fully recover. The number of those under twenty dying from cancer has risen substantially in the past few decades. Sarah Waul, a teenage girl Jonathan and his wife knew, passed away because of cancer while this book was being written. She knew Jesus as her Savior and loved Him very much. Jonathan wrote the following in *The Triumph of the Redeemed* about our receipt of brand-new bodies:

If we are alive at the time of His appearing, Jesus will instantly transform our aging and achy forms into immortal and imperishable ones. If we die before the Rapture, this is the time He will bring our dead bodies to life again and join them with our souls that are already with Him (1 Thessalonians 4:13–17).

This exchange of our dying or dead bodies for eternal, resurrected ones will be like swapping an old rusted out Ford Pinto, perhaps held together with duct tape, for a brand-new, shiny red Porsche Carrera, or perhaps a black Rolls-Royce. However, our new bodies will never deteriorate, grow old, or wear out as even the best-built and most expensive cars will do over time.

Our new bodies will forever remain immune to all sicknesses, pandemics, cancer, and any other disease you can name! This means the end of all doctor and dentist appointments (and chiropractors, too). No more vaccinations and shots! We will forget about our aches, pains, physical suffering, and the effects of aging; we'll someday regard these maladies as relics of our distant past.

What an amazing expectation! Doesn't this sure promise of an immortal and imperishable body brighten your day as you watch for Jesus' appearing? It does mine.[13]

3. The Rapture will rescue us from the presence of sin. The Rapture will initiate an eternal existence during which we will be free from the presence of sin. We all have weaknesses and sin, but oh what a fabulous day is coming when all these things will be in the past and we'll fully experience the righteousness of Christ that God has already assigned believers.

Revelation 21:4 gives us a powerful picture of what this freedom will mean:

He will wipe away every tear from their eyes, and death shall be no more, neither shall there be mourning, nor crying, nor pain anymore, for the former things have passed away.

Jesus appearing to take us home marks the beginning of a joyous and wonderful adventure. We can scarcely imagine the blessedness of the time when all the promises of this verse will be ours forever. Ponder for a moment what it will be like when we are permanently free from the presence of sin and are incapable of disobeying our Lord. Just think of the liberty that will be ours when the Lord removes all the obstacles that now limit us from being who He created us to be.

4. The Rapture will bring inner wholeness. Along with freedom from sin will come an inner wholeness such as we have never experienced. In his book *All Things New*, author and counselor John Eldredge wrote the following:

We are all traumatized and fragmented; no one passes through this vale of tears without it. And our Healer will make us whole again…. Think of it—to be wholehearted. To be filled with goodness from head to toe. To have an inner glory that matches the glory of your new body.[14]

Although the Bible doesn't specifically mention an inner restoration, we can safely assume it will happen because of what it says about our glorified bodies, the promise of 1 John 3:2–3, and the words of Revelation 21:4. There will be an amazing internal wholeness will correspond to our immortal bodies.

In this life, the Lord heals many of the wounds from our past, but not all of them. We yearn for the total inner wellness about which John Eldredge writes, don't we? In the meantime, our scars, both emotional and physical, remind us that a much better day lies ahead, the joy of being with the Savior when there will be no more sorrow, pain, sickness, or weeping forevermore.

5. The Rapture will bring joyous family reunions. At the time of the Rapture, we will see dear family members, parents, and friends who are already with Jesus in Heaven.

Jonathan's dad died when he was ten. Even at that age, he found great comfort in the words of 1 Thessalonians 4:13–17. He took a rose pedal from his father's casket and put it in his Bible to mark that passage as a reminder of his hope that he would see his dad again someday.

Imagine the reunions that will take place once Jesus takes us home to Paradise. Think of interacting with loved ones in glorified bodies that are not only free from sin, but have a youthful appearance. What will it be like to interact with them in such a remarkable state? We'll even be able to reconnect with those we're separated from by time and distance.

We realize some readers might be the only person in their earthly family taken to Heaven. Please know that in the hereafter, everyone will be family. None of us will ever feel alone or be without the love of others. Loneliness will no longer exist for any of God's children after Jesus takes us to be with Him.

6. The Rapture will fill our hearts with abundant joy. In the Upper Room on the night before His crucifixion, Jesus told His disciples:

> These things have I spoken unto you, that my joy might remain in you, and that your joy might be full. (John 15:11)

Later, the Apostle Paul would identify "joy" as one of the fruits of the Spirit (Galatians 5:22).

Yes, the Lord allows trials and storms to come into our lives. He reminds us that this world is not our home, especially during times of grief after we say goodbye to loved ones. Yet He always cares for us with the tenderness of a shepherd; He restores peace and joy to our souls through the working of the Holy Spirit.

In his book, *Morning & Evening Devotions*, Pastor David Jeremiah wrote the following about the conversion of British writer and theologian C. S. Lewis:

> C. S. Lewis's personal story in *Surprised by Joy* chronicles his journey to faith in Christ. The title reflects what he discovered: he was surprised by the joy he experienced once he received the free gift of salvation. He hadn't realized that joy would come as a result of faith.[15]

Once the Rapture happens, we will be "surprised" by a sensation of happiness greater than anything we've experienced on earth. We will wonder why we didn't spend our time focusing our minds and hearts on the ecstasy we will feel at that moment.

Thoughts of the sudden interruption to our lives might alarm us now as we think about meeting Jesus in the air. However, similar to the experience of Lewis at his conversion, exuberant delight will amaze us when we arrive on the brighter shore with our Savior. *This might be the most unexpected outcome of the Rapture of the Church.*

7. The Rapture will begin the Day of the Lord. For many, the vile wickedness, blatant injustice, widespread deception, and horrifying violence of our time are deeply troubling. There's coming a time, however, when the Lord will hand out judgment regarding these very unrighteous conditions with perfect righteousness. The words of Psalm 37:1–20 remind us that justice will someday prevail throughout the earth! We see a fuller picture of what's ahead for those who act wickedly and lead many along deadly paths in Revelation chapters 6–18.

The Rapture will begin the Day of the Lord, which includes all of the seven-year Tribulation that starts after the Rapture. Although the evil leaders of our day seem to be getting away with their disgusting schemes, the Lord will hold them all accountable.

Many folks, as exemplified by numerous posts on social media, often complain that corrupt leaders in government are getting away with their crimes. Please know this is not the case. The perfect and righteous Judge is coming, and all those who hate Him, and as a result act wickedly, will feel the full force of His wrath.

For those of us who trust Christ as Savior, the Rapture is a precious hope, because it marks the beginning of an exciting and joyous adventure that will never end. We long for the day when we'll see Jesus, and we know that once we see Him, we will be home. He's preparing a special place just for us.

Chapter 3

A HOME JUST FOR US

Whenever I am traveling, I constantly look forward to the moment when I will return home. Even if I'm very busy and preoccupied, in the back of my mind one thought is always present: "Soon I'll be going home!" Home is a place of peace and security and rest; home is where I belong. How much greater should be our longing for our eternal home! Our true home is heaven—and that is where God's path leads.

~BILLY GRAHAM, *Nearing Home*

Near the end of the classic film *The Wizard of Oz,* Dorothy repeats the phrase, "There's no place like home," as she clicks her shoes together hoping they will take her back to her beloved Kansas. Moments later, she wakes up in her bed, happy to be home again.

Even when we're sad to see our vacations end, we sense the comfort of home once we walk through the front door. The familiar surroundings have a way of putting our minds at ease. When returning from a long road trip, isn't it a great relief to begin recognizing the landscape of our region, spotting familiar landmarks, entering our city or community, and finally turning down the street that leads to home?

That's one of the many reasons for the popularity of the saying, "Home, sweet home."

When Jesus talked about the Rapture when He was in the Upper Room with His disciples, He emphasized that He was leaving to prepare a "place" for them—and for us. This will be our future, eternal residence. It will far exceed any accommodations we've enjoyed on earth, and it will, in every aspect, be "home."

Even so, we sometimes wonder about the sudden changes we'll experience when Jesus comes for us. Will we miss familiar surroundings? Will we feel homesick after the Lord takes us to a location that seems foreign? And how can we prepare for the abrupt interruption of life as we know it?

Many dread the Rapture because they may not understand that the Lord knows all about their anxious thoughts and is preparing a warm "homecoming" welcome once they arrive on the brighter shore. They may not fully trust that the Lord has their best interests in mind. If that's you, please remember the experience Terry recounted in chapter 1. After just a momentary taste of Paradise and sharing exhilaration with other saints there, he didn't even want to return to his hospital bed!

Jesus is preparing our place in Heaven with all our needs and desires in mind. Once we're there, we will instantly belong. We can trust Him to provide the best surroundings that will put our hearts at ease the moment we arrive. We will be home!

In John chapters 14–16, Jesus addressed the disciples as the future leaders of the Church. Throughout the passage, it's clear that Jesus intended for the instructions and promises to apply to all New Testament saints, as well as to His small group of followers gathered in Upper Room. Jesus mentioned His return for us (John 14:2–3) not only to the disciples, but to the apostles as well—Paul, in particular, would later receive much more information from Him about the topic.

With that in mind, let's dig a little deeper into the Lord's promise to take us to His Father's house in Heaven.

OUR HOME

The anxiety the disciples felt while with Jesus in the Upper Room didn't spring from the fact that *they* were going anywhere; it was because of the news that their beloved Master, the One whose company they had enjoyed for more than three years, would be leaving.

John 14:1–3 records the words Jesus spoke to calm their fears that evening:

> Let not your heart be troubled: ye believe in God, believe also in me. In my Father's house are many mansions: if it were not so, I would have told you. I go to prepare a place for you. And if I go and prepare a place for you, I will come again, and receive you unto myself; that where I am, there ye may be also.

Some claim Jesus wasn't talking about the Rapture in these verses, but as we examine His words and the images they would have sparked in the minds of His followers, it becomes clear that He was promising to come for them (and us) to take all of us to His "Father's house," to the "place" He's preparing for our arrival.

John 14:2–3 contains a wealth of information about our future as New Testament saints. Here are a few things we see in this passage:

1. A groom preparing a room for His Bride: The 2020 film *Before the Wrath* depicts Jewish wedding customs common in first-century Galilee. Since Jesus and His disciples grew up in that region, they were familiar with those traditions and would have recognized any references to them.

First-century AD Galilean marriages began with a betrothal ceremony witnessed by the parents of the couple and several people from the town in which they lived. The man formally proposed by offering the woman he wanted to marry a cup of wine. She signified her willingness to become his wife by *accepting* and drinking from the cup; she indicated her unwillingness to marry him by *refusing* the cup. If she accepted, her future husband took the cup back and also drank the wine, sealing their marital covenant.[16]

The disciples witnessed this custom again in the Upper Room during the Lord's Supper, when Jesus spoke the following words, as recorded in Matthew 26:27–29:

> And he took the cup, and gave thanks, and gave it to them, saying, Drink ye all of it; For this is my blood of the new testament, which is shed for many for the remission of sins. But I say unto you, I will not drink henceforth of this fruit of the vine, until that day when I drink it new with you in my Father's kingdom.

The disciples surely caught the double meaning. Not only was the Lord including them in the New Covenant promised to Israel, but, in offering them the cup of wine, He was, in essence, "proposing marriage" to the Church. The disciples accepted His proposal on our behalf by drinking from the cup before they passed it back to Jesus.

In ancient Galilee, after the groom confirmed the betrothal, he stated that he wouldn't again drink wine until the couple's wedding feast.[17] Jesus' identical promise that night in the Upper Room likely further stirred the disciples' memories of betrothal ceremonies they had witnessed (Matthew 26:29). Jesus was acting as a prospective Bridegroom of the Church, His future Bride.

With the binding marriage covenant between the man and woman in place, the groom left to prepare a room for the couple in his father's house, their future residence. The groom typically announced his intention to do so at the end of the betrothal ceremony.

When Jesus told His disciples that He was leaving to "prepare a place" for them in His "Father's house" (John 14:2–3), they would have instantly related His words to this custom. He was leaving to prepare a home for them in Heaven, just as the Jewish bridegrooms did on earth. The image of houses in Galilee with one or more such additions probably came to their minds. They knew what Jesus meant.

With the completion of the bridal chamber, the father of the groom determined its readiness and decided when to send his son to fetch his bride. Jesus twice alluded to the fact that the timing of His appearing to take us to glory, which would set off the Day of the Lord judgments, rests with the Father (Matthew 24:36; Acts 1:7).

In Jesus' day, the groom most often went to retrieve his bride in the middle of the night and amid much fanfare:

> The bridegroom would abduct his bride secretly, like a thief at night, and take her to the wedding chamber. As the bridegroom approached the bride's home, he would shout and blow the shofar (ram's horn trumpet) so that she had some warning to gather her belongings to take into the wedding chamber. The bridegroom and his friends would come into the bride's house and get the bride and her bridesmaids.[18]

Although the bride didn't know exactly when the groom would arrive, she recognized when the time was near. Once she and her bridesmaids heard the noisy procession heading their way, they emerged from her house to greet the groom and his friends.

The bride then stepped into a litter (a kind of portable couch mounted on poles), and those accompanying the groom would *lift her off the ground and carry her to the home of the groom.*[19] Just like the Jewish brides of the first century, when Jesus comes for us, His Bride, He will carry us to His Father's house in Heaven. The similarities are remarkable and unmistakable.

Brides of Jesus' day longed for the day their grooms would appear and take them back to their fathers' house. If someone had written a romance novel back then, this would've been the high point of the love story. For us, the Rapture marks the culmination of an even grander love story, that of Jesus coming for His Bride, the Church, the one for whom He gave His life on the cross to redeem. His appearing will be an equally joyous event as He quickly replaces our surprise with tears of ecstasy.

2. A physical abode: The Greek word for "place" in John 14:2-3 is *topos*, which denotes a physical location in almost all of its ninety-plus usages in the New Testament. It frequently indicates a specific location such as a city, village, or area. Jesus is preparing *actual* rooms in His Father's house for the multitudes of people who will have come to know Him as their Savior since that evening. Our new home will feature many amenities that will nicely accommodate our immortal, resurrected bodies.

The word Jesus chose for "prepare," *hetoimazo*, also depicts a tangible, visible preparation. Paul used this same term when asking Philemon to "prepare a lodging place" for him (Philemon 22). In Hebrews 11:16, the writer uses it in reference to the preparation of "a city" in reference to his promise to Abraham and Sarah of a future home.

Why the emphasis on us having a *physical* "place" in Heaven? It's because some today not only negate the promise of John 14:1–3, but also reject the idea of the New Jerusalem as being a physical city. They make the earth our eternal home, aka Heaven, with the city described in Revelation 21 merely serving as a symbol of God's presence with us. Such teaching is not only a denial of what the Bible states, but it also dims the glorious picture of Paradise that God promises us.

At the time of the Rapture, the Lord will take His followers—that is, us—to where He now resides. He made that clear in John 14:3, where He said, "where I am, there ye may be also." At the time of the Rapture, Jesus isn't coming to reside with us on earth, but to take us to heavenward so that we might see His eternal splendor, just as He requested of the Father in John 17:24:

Father, I will that they also, whom thou hast given me, be with me where I am; that they may behold my glory, which thou hast given me: for thou loved me before the foundation of the world.

The above words fit perfectly with Jesus' earlier promise in John 14:3 as well as with the words of Paul in Colossians 3:4:

When Christ, who is our life, shall appear, then shall ye also appear with him in glory.

In the Rapture, we go to be with Jesus in His heavenly abode. We don't remain on the earth, but instead witness His spectacular and magnificent existence—the one He had before He came to earth to die for our sins.

3. Our eternal home: Many saints have a faulty concept of eternity. The common portrayals of saints floating by themselves on clouds are decidedly false and unbiblical. The point of the previous discussion is to assure you that Jesus is preparing a special place, a physical abode, especially for you.

Think of the great care and tender love of a first-century groom preparing a room for himself and his bride. Now transfer to thoughts of Jesus, who is right now preparing our forever home with all our needs and desires in mind. Furthermore, He has no limitations regarding how He constructs it and what He provides for us in it.

We believe our future residence in New Jerusalem will forever be the place we call home. Most certainly, we will return to earth with Jesus at His Second Coming and will have roles in ruling with Him over the nations during the Millennium and then in the eternal state. However, the place Jesus is now preparing for us will be our primary residence.

The New Jerusalem will exceed even our most fanciful expectations;

it will be the most beautiful place imaginable, and it will be ours along with the redeemed of all the ages. The God who created all the wonders and gorgeous views in our world dwells there forever. That alone makes all our grandest thoughts of the spectacle of this city feeble by comparison. How can it not be a place of spectacular wonder? How can we expect anything less from the habitation we will share with the Lord?

4. The nature of our glorified bodies: Now that we've examined the dwelling Jesus is preparing for us, we can briefly return to the matter of the glorified bodies we will have while residing there. In Philippians 3:20–21, Paul wrote:

> But our citizenship is in heaven, and from it we await a Savior, the Lord Jesus Christ, who will transform our lowly body to be like his glorious body, by the power that enables him even to subject all things to himself.

Once Jesus transforms us at His appearing, our bodies will closely resemble His resurrected one. Pastor and author David Jeremiah referred to these as the "prototype of the ones we'll have throughout eternity." He then added:

> Some things about Jesus' glorified body were similar to the one He had before He died. He resembled Himself; He could eat and drink; He could be touched. Yet He could pass through walls, and He appeared in various places without traveling by recognized means.[20]

We don't know if we will have all the capabilities Jesus had, such as the ability to appear to the disciples behind locked doors or become invisible at will. However, our bodies will be supernatural in many respects, especially in comparison to our earthly ones. For instance, we will be able to travel effortlessly and perhaps instantly between Heaven and the earth in order to fulfill the responsibilities Jesus will give us during His reign.

Imagine! Our eternal existence will be more joy-filled and exciting than anything our minds can even invent. Our ability to move back and forth between the heavenly and earthly realms will amaze us, as will our capacity to freely move about on the earth.

A HOME THAT WILL NEVER DISAPPOINT

We will dwell forever in a home that will never disappoint us throughout eternity. Can you even begin to picture a place so wonderful that, even after living there for ten thousand years, it will still bring great satisfaction and warmth? Doesn't that exceed all your wildest thoughts?

Because we're limited in our ability to understand our immortal bodies and the details of life in eternity, we often find it hard to fathom how a place can be so glorious and enjoyable—forever. Much of the blame for this difficulty we have lies with the pagan philosopher Plato, who had a profound, yet tragic, influence on the history of the Church. Because of him, many Christians believe that expecting physical pleasures in eternity is sinful, and that Heaven will only offer us "spiritual" blessings. Such a spiritualization of our coming blessings couldn't be farther from the truth.

When Jesus comes for us, as we've said, He will take us to the dwelling He has prepared specifically for us with all the love that took Him to the cross so He could give us eternal life. We will enjoy His beauty and splendor for all time. There will be tangible pleasures for our senses that will cause us to praise our Lord all the more.

In Heaven, we will feast with the saints of all the ages, delight in the place Jesus is preparing for us, never tire of the city in which we will dwell, and always adore the majestic scenes of the New Earth.

Christian songwriter and artist Chris Tomlin's 2016 album, "Never Lose Sight," features a track entitled "Home." The words poetically and powerfully describe the desire we all have to leave this world's pain and suffering behind to arrive at "a better place" of freedom and joy in the Lord's "open arms" in Heaven.[21]

If anything causes us to long for our heavenly home all the more, it's the presence of wickedness, lawlessness, violence, and the tsunami of deception we see everywhere in our world. All these conditions are setting the stage for the coming Tribulation and the rule of Antichrist. We believe the leading figures in that prophesied time are ready and waiting for the curtain to rise on their quest for world domination.

In the two chapters that follow, we will contrast the future of this world with incredible joys set before us in the hereafter.

Chapter 4

COLLIDING KINGDOMS

We are living in an age when everything, including reality itself, is being redefined in order to conform to a godless worldview and its value system. But as far reaching as this values hijacking is, do not think for a moment that Satan is satisfied. On the contrary, he has his sights set on an even greater goal—to rule the world. Nothing short of sitting in Earth's pilot seat will do for him.[22]

~MARK HITCHCOCK AND JEFF KINLEY, *Global Reset*

I t's the tower of Babel all over again.

The New World Order architects claim the ability to make life on earth better than the one humankind has thus far managed to construct. The slogan for those who preach this hope of a future utopia is "Build back better!" The name they give the result of their reconstruction project is the "Great Reset."

In making their grandiose plans, today's powerbrokers make the same deliberate, monumental mistake the ancients made in Genesis 11. Led by Nimrod, they sought to build a city and a tower. They thought the latter would protect them against another worldwide flood.

These early would-be masters of planet earth, like their father Lucifer, determined to usurp the throne of God. They desired to be like the

Most High God—take the place of the Creator. They fell for Satan's lie that they could be like Him.

This time we don't see a tall structure stretching heavenward, but rather the World Economic Forum (WEF) led by Klaus Schwab and his closest advisor, Yuval Harari. The intent of opposing God and uniting the world under a Satanic regime, however, is the same as in Genesis 11.

During the week of January 16–20, 2023, the WEF held its annual meeting in Davos. Switzerland. The event drew more than 2,700 attendees consisting of 50 heads of state, 380 top government officials, scores of powerful corporate CEOs, and several other elite dignitaries.

Although their intent sounded benign on the surface, the goal of uniting the people of the world under the banner of "Build back better" is Satanic, deadly, and reminiscent of Genesis 11.

Leo Hohmann, blogger and investigative reporter, wrote this about the WEF's attempt to solve the world's problems, most of which they themselves engineered:

> But now the stakes are higher because more of us regular folks are waking up and learning about the true agenda of the WEF's Great Reset and Fourth Industrial Revolution. They intend to digitally enslave the world in a total surveillance state based on a global digital ID (likely disguised as vaccine passports) and a global digital currency to replace cash….
>
> *The WEF bemoans the current economic reality in its Global Risks Report, ignoring the fact that most of the economic problems were caused by the very elites who now propose to have the solutions.*[23]
> (Emphasis added)

The Luciferin determination of the globalists at the WEF and UN, through their sin-infected, upside-down thinking, will succeed for a short while. During the seven-year Tribulation, similar to the builders of the ill-fated Tower of Babel, these elite seek to unite the world under the banner of a one-world government only to run afoul of the same God who will destroy both them and their kingdom.

The builders of the ancient city and tower hoped to "make a name for" themselves (Genesis 11:4). Given the advanced age of many of those pushing to reenact the uniting of all people under one banner, that's a desire they possess as well. If that's true, these elite members of the geriatrics ward will not like the outcome the Lord has in store for them. In Psalm 34:11, we read:

> The face of the Lord is against them that do evil, to cut off the remembrance of them from the earth.

Not only will the Lord destroy their kingdom, but no one will remember their names once He establishes His realm on the earth. What a wonderful thought!

Make no mistake, we're witnessing the beginnings of the implementation of the final form of worldwide wickedness. It's a time when Satan's kingdom is colliding with God's rule. The good news for us as believers is that we will be going home in the near future.

MODERN-DAY TOWER OF BABEL

In the book of Ephesians, Paul refers to the invisible nature of the forces that currently oppose us and exercise dominion in our current world (2:1–3; 6:12). The WEF, combined with the UN and its Agenda 2030, represents the devil's renewed attempt to form a worldwide government that will coerce submission to the devil's destructive and deadly agenda. He desires a more visible and oppressive empire that will enslave humanity.

The majority of people don't want the global governance Schwab and his cronies advocate. Business magnate and billionaire Elon Musk asked people on the social media platform formerly known as "Twitter" (now known as "X," which he now owns) whether the WEF should "control the world." With well over two million votes, 86 percent said, "No." While not a scientific poll, it demonstrated that a large majority don't want what the WEF is peddling.

Regardless of popular opinion, the elite globalists are well on their way to reaching their goal of world governance. Below are just some of the things they're doing to impose their will upon an unsuspecting humanity:

1. An essential step in gaining control over the nations is reducing the world's population. We see this through the horrors of abortion, the LGBTQ+ attack on children causing gender confusion, and the mRNA injections that are increasing infertility and killing people at an ever-increasing rate, yet so few see these things for what they are.

2. Central Bank Digital Currencies (CBDCs) are another way the globalists will later seize control of people through something they will initially believe is beneficial. More than one hundred nations either already have digital currencies or are considering them. In America, it may come through FedNow, the digital currency the Federal Reserve in America introduced in the summer of 2023.

3. Transhumanism, which the WEF refers to as the "Fourth Industrial Revolution," is a priority for them, and they are much farther along with it than most anyone can even imagine. Their stated objective in this, via Yuval Harari, is to eliminate human free will. They will accomplish this through the use of pharmaceuticals.

4. The "Pandemic Treaty," if approved by member nations of the World Health Organization (WHO), would give the head of the WHO sovereign powers over all member nations to declare

health emergencies with restrictions and vaccinations enforceable with military might. Only a handful of people see the danger here for what it is.

The widespread acceptance of these four things, even by most who oppose the WEF agenda, tells us just how close the world is to the formation of Antichrist's kingdom. The stage is already set, and many of the actors are in place awaiting the raising of the curtain.

When God Says, "Enough!"

As we watch today's world moving closer to the enslavement envisioned by the globalists, we know that someday soon God will say, "Enough!" The following words of the Lord Jesus in Luke 17:28–30 foreshadow that heavenly exclamation:

> Likewise, just as it was in the days of Lot—they were eating and drinking, buying and selling, planting and building, but on the day when Lot went out from Sodom, fire and sulfur rained from heaven and destroyed them all—so will it be on the day when the Son of Man is revealed. (ESV)

At that time, the Lord will remove God's children from the earth, just as He did Lot (whom He saw as righteous because of Lot's belief in the Lord) from the wicked city of Sodom before He destroyed it (Genesis 19). Here is how our removal from this wicked world will happen, according to God's Holy Word:

> For the Lord himself shall descend from heaven with a shout, with the voice of the archangel, and with the trump of God: and the dead in Christ shall rise first: Then we which are alive

and remain shall be caught up together with them in the clouds, to meet the Lord in the air: and so shall we ever be with the Lord. Wherefore comfort one another with these words" (1 Thessalonians 4:16–18)

Jesus will appear to take us home at a time when life seems normal, just as it was for the people of Sodom on the day God destroyed the city. For the world, it's business as usual until the Lord says, "No more," and begins pouring out His wrath in order to reclaim the nations from the grasp of Satan. For us as New Testament saints, we dare not think any sense of normalcy will continue for long. Instead, we should anticipate Jesus' soon appearing to take us home to glory. We already see the great clash of kingdoms through which the Lord will allow Antichrist to rule for short while.

JESUS CRUSHES ANTICHRIST'S KINGDOM

Twenty-six hundred years ago, Daniel predicted the demise of Satan's kingdom, the one we see forming before our eyes. In a dream about the world powers that would come after his, King Nebuchadnezzar saw "a stone" that "struck the image on its feet of iron and clay and broke them in pieces" (Daniel 2:34). In his interpretation of the dream, the prophet spoke these words to the king in Daniel 2:44:

And in the days of those kings the God of heaven will set up a kingdom that shall never be destroyed, nor shall the kingdom be left to another people. It shall break in pieces all these kingdoms and bring them to an end, and it shall stand forever.

When God's kingdom comes to the earth at the Second Coming, Jesus will destroy all the world's realms under the power of the devil through Antichrist. This didn't happen at Pentecost, as some today mistakenly claim, and Christ didn't assign the Church the task of world domination. He alone will crush the powerbrokers of Satan at His return.

The globalists believe they can rule over the world, but in reality they're preparing the way for Jesus to bring God's great kingdom to earth with the most amazing display of power, glory, and magnificence the world has ever seen.

And, as those in Christ, we will have a front row seat for it.

Before that happens, however, the world must experience the Tribulation, which will occur between the Rapture and Jesus' visible return to earth.

Chapter 5

HEAVEN'S GLORY VS. TRIBULATION TERRORS

For then shall be great tribulation, such as was not since the beginning of the world to this time, no, nor ever shall be. And except those days should be shortened, there should no flesh be saved: but for the elect's sake those days shall be shortened.

~Jesus, Matthew 24:21–22

God's Word is a book of supernatural and stark contrasts: good versus evil, salvation versus being lost, God versus Satan—all related in the same way, by examining the individual soul's position in regard to God's Holy order.

The great contrast we will briefly look at here is the profound difference between the horrendous period of Tribulation that Jesus said will be the worst time of all human history (Matthew 24:21–22) versus the post-Rapture era in Heaven for all the saints of the Church Age, which will be full of praise, thanksgiving, celebration, and glorious wonders beyond what we can imagine.

Looking deeply into biblical eschatology, the study of future things, moves us quickly into John's Revelation and his prophecies concerning the time of God's judgments on the earth followed by Jesus' millennial reign and the wonders of the eternal state.

RAPTURE BEFORE THE TRIBULATION

God's Word makes it clear for anyone who honestly explores prophecy that the Church will not be present during the Tribulation. This is evident from the book of Revelation, which the Apostle John divided into three parts, as recorded in Revelation 1:19:

Write the things which thou hast seen, and the things which are, and the things which shall be hereafter.

Notice the breakdown:

1. The "things which thou hast seen": This refers to the vision of Christ in Revelation chapter 1.
2. The "things which are": This consists of Jesus' messages to the seven churches as recorded in Revelation chapters 2 and 3. These represent the present Church Age.
3. The "things which shall be hereafter": This includes all that's unveiled in Revelation chapters 4–22.

When John began to reveal the things that will be our hereafter, his words of introduction in 4:1 show that he was starting his third major division, for the chapter opens with "hereafter" (Greek: *meta houtos*). The emphasis is on what the Lord will reveal "after this," the events following the Church Age.

Once the Lord caught John up to Heaven, he saw a throne and a heavenly being occupying the throne. Also sitting on thrones are twenty-four beings described as "elders." Their position, activities, and words display a special relationship of the Church to this group. The identification of these twenty-four elders tells us how the Church relates to the events of the Tribulation period.

The Elders

In Israel, the elders were representatives of the people, but far more in importance, they were judges of the people. They were God's ordained ministers in rendering judgment upon those who belonged to God's chosen nation. They had a significant relationship with God in the exercise of judgment.

The elders in Revelation 4 and 5 who enter in connection with God's throne are, like God, enthroned. They are identified with Him in the judgment that Heaven will soon execute upon the Earth.

Walter Scott, in his book, *Exposition of the Revelation of Jesus Christ*, wrote the following about the elders:

> "Elders" as a term occurs twelve times. The varied actions and services in which they take part show clearly enough that they are the representatives of the redeemed and risen saints. They are enthroned, fall down and worship; one of them comforts the weeping Seer and interprets the mind of heaven; they have harps, and vials of incense; they sing (never said of angels); are the nearest company to the throne and to the Lamb; intelligently explain as to the redeemed on earth; celebrate the millennial and eternal triumph of God; and add their "amen" and "hallelujah" to the judgment of the whore—the corruptress of the earth."[24]

After quoting the above words of Scott, theologian Dwight Pentecost added these words in his book *Things to Come*:

> An examination of the passages in which their activities are mentioned will emphasize the fact that the elders give worship and glory to God as each new step in the plan of God to establish His kingdom and overthrow the kingdom of the evil one is unfolded before them.[25]

Many pre-Tribulation scholars and students, as did Dr. Pentecost, regard the "hereafter" referred to in Revelation 4:1 as the eternal kingdom of God, which includes all believers transported into His presence through the Rapture of the Church. The twenty-four elders represent the raptured Church in Heaven before the time of wrath described in Revelation 6–18 begins.

The judgments for those left behind will be catastrophic beyond comprehension. God's Word, specifically the book of Revelation, explains this coming time of God's fury in great detail. It describes twenty-one specific judgments in a series of seven scroll judgments, seven trumpet judgments, and seven bowl judgments.

KEY EVENTS RELATED TO THE TRIBULATION

With this framework in mind, let's look at how these things will unfold on God's prophetic timeline.

1. The Rapture of the Church

While the storm clouds of apocalypse gather and approach, Christians attuned to God's Word should pay attention to the signs. They must be aware of the elements of that approaching storm of Tribulation. Things of society and cultures in every endeavor of life will, at the same time, seem to be going about business as usual. At the moment of the Lord's next intervention into humankind's affairs, times will be like they were in the days of Noah and Lot (read Luke 17:26–30). It will be a catastrophic involvement in the lives of humanity.

Jesus will step out on the clouds and shout, "Come up here!" (Revelation 4:1–2). All Christians—those who accept Christ's blood atonement for salvation (born-again believers) will instantly be with Jesus above the earth (see 1 Corinthians 15:51–55 and 1 Thessalonians 4:13–18). Tens of millions of people, if not many more, will suddenly vanish; they will disappear from the planet before the astonished eyes of those left behind. The Lord will take His Church, all believers since the Day of Pentecost, back to Heaven, where He has prepared a place of eternal dwelling for them (John 14:1–3). In the next chapter, we describe the judgment seat of Christ where we will receive rewards for our faithful service.

As the Church celebrates in Heaven, things on earth will rapidly deteriorate as Antichrist makes his appearance on the world scene.

2. Antichrist Deceives Many

The world's nations will be in chaos after the Rapture. The turmoil will cause severe ramifications as governments seek to restore civil order and regain governmental and economic equilibrium. Dramatic shifts of power will take place among the nations. According to Bible prophecy, one man will step forward to proffer a plan to quell the fears of war in the Middle East (Daniel 9:27). This prophecy correlates to Revelation 6:2, with the rider on the white horse bringing people under his control (Revelation 6:2).

The new world leader, the "man of lawlessness" (2 Thessalonians 2:3–7), will arrive just in time to appear to be a knight in shining armor. He will have the answer to the looming all-out war in the Middle East. He will be able to sell a seven-year peace plan that is already available, apparently.

Israel will agree to the covenant, as will its enemies, and, in effect, the entire world will accept the European leader's masterful sales pitch.

However, Israel's acceptance will fly in the face of God. Isaiah 28:18 describes the covenant this way:

> And your covenant with death shall be disannulled, and your agreement with hell shall not stand; when the overflowing scourge shall pass through, then ye shall be trodden down by it.

God will not tolerate their deal with the devil; it will cause His judgmental wrath to fall on His people.

The pact with Israel will reveal Antichrist as the prophesied "man of lawlessness". This world leader will suffer a deadly head wound around the midpoint of the Tribulation (Revelation 13:3). However, he will be resurrected (supposedly from death) and with Satan totally indwelling and empowering him.

He will demand worship from all of the world's inhabitants and cause all to accept his mark; otherwise, he will cut them out of the economic system—preventing them from engaging in any buying and selling (Revelation 13). He will kill those who refuse to worship him. The chief method of death-dealing will be beheading.

The regime of Antichrist will, at its beginning, consist of ten kingdoms, whose newly crowned kings (political leaders of the region) will later give him all of their authority and power. He will bring together one world government, one world economy, and one world religion, to some extent—for a brief time, at least. This will be a Babylonian-type system that will all but enslave the entire world.

3. Tribulation Evangelism

During the Tribulation, a multitude of martyred believers will appear in Heaven before God's throne (Revelation 6:9–11, 7:9–17). As a part of the Church in Heaven, it's likely we will witness the scene of the Tribulation saints pleading their case before the Father.

With the Church absent from the earth, the Lord will use other means to proclaim the Gospel.

The Lord will not allow the dark, Satanic realm to go unchallenged. God will seal (protect from Satan and his minions) 144,000 Jewish men whom we believe will share the saving message of Jesus Christ with the world (Revelation 7:3–8). Millions upon millions of people will hear the message and become Christians during the Tribulation period. This will result in multitudes of believers being killed by Antichrist.

God will also place two Jewish men in Jerusalem during this time for the purpose of preaching the Gospel and pointing the finger of judgment at those whose repentance isn't forthcoming. No one knows for sure who these men will be, but there seems good evidence that at least one of them will be Elijah, the Old Testament prophet whom God took up from earth in a fiery whirlwind. Others speculate the second one will be Moses.

The Satanic governmental regime will seek to eliminate the pair, but won't be able to do so until God allows. Anyone who tries to kill them will, in like manner, experience death, according to the prophetic Word. Finally, the regime will murder them. Their dead bodies will lie in the streets of Jerusalem for three days, after which God will resurrect them and lift them into the sky before the astonished eyes of their murderers and the entire world (Revelation 11:1–13).

4. Persecution of the Jews

Jesus said the Jews who will occupy Jerusalem during the Tribulation will flee at the sight of Antichrist defiling the Jewish temple (Matthew 24:15–20). This era, beginning at the midpoint of the seven-year Tribulation, will begin the "time of Jacob's trouble" (Jeremiah 30: 7)—a time Jesus says will be the worst in all history (Matthew 24:21).

Zechariah 13:8–9 states that two-thirds of the Jewish people living in Israel will perish, presumably by the hand of Antichrist. We believe Revelation 12:13–17 refers to God's protection of the Israelites who flee from the evil leader's wrath.

Out of great suffering will come a gloriously restored kingdom for Israel. The surviving Jewish people will repent just before Jesus' return to earth and go into the realm in their natural bodies.

5. Worldwide Devastation and Death

Revelation chapters 6–18 describe twenty-one specific judgments in a series of seven scroll (or seal) judgments, seven trumpet judgments, and seven bowl judgments. The first two sets of catastrophes will kill over half the world's population. By the end of the Tribulation, humanity will be on the edge of extinction (Matthew 24:22).

Not only that, but the disasters God sends upon the earth will devastate the eco-systems of the world. The Lord will respond to today's worshipers of nature by wreaking havoc on the environment. In chapter 10, we will look at Jesus' restoration of creation back to its pristine original condition at the start of the Millennium.

In Isaiah 26:20–21, we find the following account of the Lord's fury during this coming day:

> Come, my people, enter your chambers, and shut your doors behind you; hide yourselves for a little while until the fury has passed by.
>
> For behold, the Lord is coming out from his place to punish the inhabitants of the earth for their iniquity, and the earth will disclose the blood shed on it, and will no more cover its slain.

It's clear that this passage refers to the Day of the Lord judgments, which John further described in Revelation 6–18, but who are the ones the Lord instructs to "enter your chambers?" Could this be the Church in Heaven? Many believe it is, especially because of the reference to a resurrection of the dead in Isaiah 26:19. If so, and we think it's quite probable, this fits with what we looked at in the previous chapter, as the "chambers" would refer to the dwelling places the Lord is preparing for us.

6. The Battle of Armageddon

At the end of the Tribulation, the armies of the world come together in the land of Israel for the Battle of Armageddon. The devil will bring them together with diverse motives, but his main desire will be to stop Jesus' glorious return and prevent Him from setting up His thousand-year reign over the earth centered in Jerusalem.

The kings of the east, with their vast army, will march toward a rendezvous with all other nations of the world:

> For, behold, in those days, and in that time, when I shall bring again the captivity of Judah and Jerusalem, I will also gather all nations, and will bring them down into the valley of Jehoshaphat, and will plead with them there for my people and for my heritage Israel, whom they have scattered among the nations, and parted my land. (Joel 3:1–2).

Just as the battle is becoming so violent that it threatens the end of all people and animals on earth, the black clouds of apocalypse unroll like a scroll, and brilliant light from heaven's core breaks through, revealing the King of kings and His armies and myriad angelic hosts.

In Revelation 19:11–15, we have John's eyewitness account of the Lord Jesus preparing to intervene in this great battle:

> And I saw heaven opened, and behold a white horse; and he that sat upon him was called Faithful and True, and in

righteousness he doth judge and make war. His eyes were as a flame of fire, and on his head were many crowns; and he had a name written, that no man knew, but he himself. And he was clothed with a vesture dipped in blood: and his name is called The Word of God. And the armies which were in heaven followed him upon white horses, clothed in fine linen, white and clean. And out of his mouth goeth a sharp sword, that with it he should smite the nations: and he shall rule them with a rod of iron: and he treadeth the winepress of the fierceness and wrath of Almighty God.

WHY DISCUSS THE TRIBULATION?

You might be wondering why we would include chapters on the coming kingdom of Antichrist and the Tribulation in a book about the hereafter. Won't the Church be in Heaven during this time, away from the destruction on earth?

First, our purpose is to show the extreme contrast between our joyful experiences in glory versus those of the ones who are left behind at the time of the Rapture. This will be by far the worst time of human history.

Second, when we compare world events to biblical prophecy, we see that we live in the last hours of human history as we know it. (See appendix B for a list of the signs pointing to the soon arrival of the Tribulation and hence to the Rapture that precedes it.)

Third, and most importantly, it gives us an opportunity to present the saving message of the cross. For those who reject Christ's sacrifice, the Tribulation is only a part of the terror that awaits.

Yes, a large multitude of people will turn to the Savior during this time; however, Antichrist, along with the false religious leader of this time, will kill the majority of those who do.

You don't want to wait until then to trust the Lord with your eternal destiny. Furthermore, you may not survive the chaos that will immediately follow the Rapture.

John 3:16 says:

For God so loved the world, that he gave his only Son, that whoever believes in him should not perish but have eternal life.

Jesus died in our place so we might receive eternal life rather than perish during the coming Tribulation and endure an eternity in Hell without Him. Jesus said simply believe in Him and we will receive eternal life. The Apostle Paul, as recorded in Romans 10:13, said:

For everyone who calls on the name of the Lord will be saved.

If you've never called out to the Lord in faith, please do so today.

Many people know all about Jesus and admire His teachings, but reject His offer of forgiveness for their sins. Instead, they depend on themselves, on their own way of approaching God. They mistakenly think they can bypass Jesus and still get to Heaven based on their own goodness, sincerity, family heritage, or generic belief in God.

They cannot.

Jesus said:

I am the way, and the truth, and the life. No one comes to the Father except through me. (John 14:6)

Saving faith is absolutely exclusive; Jesus is the one and only path to eternal life.

Is Jesus your Savior? Do you trust Him alone for eternal life? If so, you will go to Paradise with Him when He comes for His Church.

When Christ, who is our life, shall appear, then shall ye also appear with him in glory. (Colossians 3:4)

Please don't delay in putting your trust in Jesus. Call upon Him today.

Chapter 6

REWARDS BEYOND IMAGINATION

According to the Bible, the all-knowing, all-seeing God is keeping track of how you're living and what you're doing for Him every day...Rewards for serving Christ faithfully are beyond our wildest imagination.[26]

~MARK HITCHCOCK, *Heavenly Rewards*

Amid the daily grind, we're often tempted to think our efforts to please the Lord won't matter much beyond this life. We might ask questions such as: "Is my endless toil at the office pleasing to the Lord?" "Does He see how much I love my spouse?" "Will Jesus reward my service for Him no matter how insignificant it might seem?" The answer to all these questions is a resounding "Yes!"

Just after he expresses our hope of receiving immortal bodies at the time of the Rapture (1 Corinthians 15:58), the Apostle Paul offers these encouraging words:

Therefore, my beloved brothers, be steadfast, immovable, always abounding in the work of the Lord, knowing that in the Lord your labor is not in vain. (ESV)

The Lord sees and will reward us for all we do for Him. Yes, there are other reasons to serve, such as our love for the Savior, a response for all He's done for us, and a desire to bless others. These don't diminish the motivation that comes from looking ahead to the rewards the Lord will give us for faithfully serving Him.

If you still wonder if such a focus might be self-centered, please read the following from author Mark Hitchcock:

> Because rewarding believers is God's idea, disregarding or denying eternal rewards is an insult to our gracious Father. The rewards God offers us are priceless treasures that He expects us to desire....
>
> Rewards are a big deal to God, and someday, when we stand before Him, they will be a big deal to us as well. They will be tangible evidence that we pleased the Lord with our life. For that reason, they should be important to us now, because this is the only season during which we can earn them.[27]

It's not wrong to think about rewards; they should motivate us to follow His lead and serve Him in whatever capacity He calls us.

JUDGMENT SEAT OF CHRIST

After the Rapture, we will appear before the judgment seat of Christ to give an account of our lives and hear Jesus' assessment of our service for Him. This time of examination will happen to New Testament saints—all those living in the Church Age prior to Jesus' appearing. Paul introduced us to this event in 2 Corinthians 5:10:

> For we must all appear before the judgment seat of Christ; that every one may receive the things done in his body, according to that he hath done, whether it be good or bad.

While this sounds a bit scary, a couple of factors make it much less daunting:

1. The Lord has already forgiven all of our sins. Jesus won't judge our sins; He's already paid the debt for them in our place. He has forever removed them from us. We will stand before Him "holy and without blame" (Ephesians 1:4) on that day. This time of examination occurs *after* we arrive in Heaven with immortal and sinless bodies. This isn't an exam we have to pass to gain entry to Paradise; it's a time of receiving rewards for our service to our Master.

Dr. Dwight Pentecost, well-known author and former beloved professor at Dallas Theological Seminary, wrote that the word Paul used for "bad" in 2 Corinthians 5:10 is not the term the apostle typically used to indicate morally wrong, sinful behavior:

> Thus the judgment is not to determine what is ethically good or evil, but rather that which is worthless. It is not the Lord's purpose here to chasten His child for his sins, but to reward his service for those things done in the name of the Lord.[28]

In 2 Corinthians 5:21, the apostle wrote this:

> For he hath made him to be sin for us, who knew no sin; that we might be made the righteousness of God in him."

As redeemed saints, we are forever righteous in God's sight.

Late author and Bible scholar Ed Hindson put it this way in his book, *Future Glory*:

> One of the many blessings of trusting in Jesus now is that we will face only one judgment—the judgment seat of Christ. This judgment will not determine whether or not we enter heaven,

but it will determine our rewards in eternity. How you live your life as a believer today will determine how God blesses your life for eternity.[29]

2. The Greek word *bema* denotes rewards, not punishment. The Greek word Paul uses for "judgment seat" in 2 Corinthians 5:10 is *bema*. In his day, the term referred to a raised seat or platform that served a variety of functions. It appears most often in connection with the ancient Ishmian games, the forerunner of our modern Olympics.

From an elevated position, or *bema*, a judge presided over the competition to ensure that everyone participated according to the rules. At the completion of the athletic contests, the raised podium became a visible place for that official to hand out crowns to the winners.

In his commentary on 2 Corinthians, pastor and author John MacArthur wrote the following about the *bema*:

> Judgment seat translates *bema*, which, in its simplest definition, describes a place reached by steps, or a platform.... In Greek culture bema referred to the elevated platform on which victorious athletes received their crowns, much like the medal stand in the modern Olympic games.[30]

Will other believers witness the time of judgment we spend with the Savior? The Bible doesn't tell us that directly, but the ancient usage of *bema* makes it a distinct possibility that other saints will celebrate our rewards with us.

The Apostle Paul said that our time before the Lord will also include our assessment of our own lives:

> So then every one of us shall give account of himself to God. (Romans 14:12)

So not only will the Lord review our lives, but we also will offer an evaluation of our service and relationship with Him.

WHEN WILL THE BEMA OCCUR?

First Corinthians 4:5 verifies that the *bema* will take place after the "Lord comes," so we know it will occur after the Rapture. Dwight Pentecost, in the excerpt below, connects the dots placing the *bema* after the Lord takes His redeemed home to glory but before the Second Coming:

> In 1 Corinthians 4:5; 2 Timothy 4:8, and Revelation 22:12 the reward is associated with "that day," that is, the day in which He comes for His own. Thus it must be observed that the rewarding of the church must take place between the rapture and the revelation of Christ to the earth.[31]

With our limited perspective of eternity versus time, this presents a logistical problem. How can Jesus examine all of those who have died in fellowship with Him since the Day of Pentecost as well as the multitudes of living saints He will have just caught up to Heaven in the Rapture—all in just seven years? It would take much longer than that for just a million believers to stand before Him and have their entire lives analyzed for a mere hour.

We must, however, recognize that our sovereign and all-powerful God is not bound by time. As such, is it not possible for Jesus to complete this task without any time passing on the earth? It's impossible for us to comprehend an existence outside the constraints of time. The passing of seconds, minutes, days, weeks, etc., is all we know, which prevents us from fully understanding our relationship to time in eternity when such things will not matter.

A book that became a popular movie might help us grasp how the *bema* can take place without a moment of time passing on earth.

In *The Lion, the Witch and the Wardrobe*, a fantasy novel written by C. S. Lewis, young characters named Peter, Susan, Edmund, and Lucy Pevensie journey to another realm, Narnia, through a mysterious and magical wardrobe. Once there, the siblings rescue Narnia from an evil witch who had plunged the realm into a one-hundred-year winter. Aslan, who represents Jesus in the narrative, then anoints the children as kings and queens for their efforts in the rescue.

After the four became adults and had reigned in Narnia for many years, they unintentionally passed through the wardrobe again. They become children again without even one minute having passed at their home during the lengthy time they had been away.

That's how we envision the judgment seat of Christ. The Lord will supernaturally transport us outside the earthly dimension of time to complete the examination and hand out rewards.

This would explain how the twenty-four elders, who represent the Church in Heaven, are able to "cast their crowns" before God's throne (Revelation 4:10) before the start of the Tribulation judgments recorded in the book of Revelation (6:1).

What Will Happen at the Bema?

In 1 Corinthians 3:10–15, Paul provides insight about what will happen when we appear before the judgment seat of Christ:

According to the grace of God given to me, like a skilled master builder I laid a foundation, and someone else is building upon it. Let each one take care how he builds upon it. For no one can lay a foundation other than that which is laid, which is Jesus Christ. Now if anyone builds on the foundation with gold, silver, precious stones, wood, hay, straw—each one's work will become manifest, for the Day will disclose it, because it will be revealed by fire, and the fire will test what sort of work each one has done. If the work that anyone has built on the foundation survives, he will receive a reward. If anyone's work is burned up, he will suffer loss, though he himself will be saved, but only as through fire. (ESV)

Jesus will assess our "works" by fire and reward us for the ones that withstand the blaze. Some will watch as the flames devour everything, and although they will remain in Heaven, they will regret missing rewards that might have been theirs. It's possible that their works were more self-honoring than Christ-glorifying, failed to appropriate the gifts the Lord gave them, or were not based on Scripture.

Works based on the "foundation" of Jesus will survive the fiery test and become the basis for our rewards. In Ephesians 2:20, the apostle wrote:

And are built upon the foundation of the apostles and prophets, Jesus Christ himself being the chief corner stone.

The Bible is thus the ultimate guide for our service to the Lord.

Matthew 24:14–30 records Jesus' parable of the talents. Those who prove to be good stewards of what the Lord gives them will hear their Master say:

Well done, good and faithful servant; thou hast been faithful over a few things, I will make thee ruler over many things: enter thou into the joy of thy lord. (Matthew 24:23 23)

The Lord will reward those who have faithfully used the gifts, talents, and opportunities He provides. For many, hearing the Savior express His approval of our lives will be just as precious as the crowns— or even more so.

LOOKING FORWARD TO THE BEMA:
JONATHAN'S WORDS

Looking forward to the *bema* is not a matter of overconfidence, but a desire to hear the Lord's true assessment of my service on His behalf. As with many who write about biblical prophecy, I often encounter fierce criticism because of what I believe about the Rapture and the Lord's restoration of a kingdom for Israel. It's not that I doubt what the Bible says about these things—not at all. But I sometimes wonder if my writing on these topics has genuinely pleased the Lord. Has my critique of others who don't believe what Scripture says about these things been too harsh? Are my motives truly pleasing to the Lord?

I long to hear what the Lord has to say about my service, even if it's less favorable than I expect. The words of Paul in 1 Corinthians 13:12 come to mind:

> For now we see through a glass, darkly; but then face to face: now I know in part; but then shall I know even as also I am known.

When we stand before Jesus, it will be a face-to-face encounter that will bring much joy, of course, but also a true and comprehensive assessment of our service on His behalf.

As someone whose love language is primarily words, hearing the words, "Well done, good and faithful servant," is most important to me. However, perhaps by that day, the matter of crowns will loom larger in my mind.

CROWNS

The Bible refers to five specific crowns the Lord will award members of His Church. These are not, however, the type monarchs wore in ancient times, but rather the kind victorious athletes received.

J. Dwight Pentecost describes the difference between the two types of crowns:

> Thus the very word Paul chooses to describe the rewards is that associated with honor and dignity bestowed on the overcomer. Although we will reign with Christ, the kingly crown is His alone. The victor's crowns are ours.[32]

While we were finishing up this book in May of 2023, Charles III was crowned as king of the United Kingdom. Two crowns were used at the widely publicized coronation, with the media emphasizing their dazzling appearance, historic significance, and the number of precious stones on each one. Our crowns will look much different than the ones placed on the King of England's head (thankfully!), and they will glorify our Lord rather than ourselves.

Our future crowns will provide a strong connection between our current faithfulness and the responsibilities Jesus assigns to us in the hereafter. The act of casting our crowns before the Lord (Revelation 4:10) will signify our awareness that they came as a result of Jesus working through us and not by our own efforts.

Here are brief descriptions of the five crowns mentioned in the New Testament:

1. The Imperishable Crown: Ed Hindson, in *Future Glory*, said Jesus will give an imperishable crown "to those who exhibit faithful endurance through trials."[33] Paul described this reward in 1 Corinthians 9:24–25 by setting it in the context of competing for a prize in the contests of his day:

> Every athlete exercises self-control in all things. They do it to receive a perishable wreath, but we an imperishable. So I do not run aimlessly; I do not box as one beating the air. But I discipline

my body and keep it under control, lest after preaching to others I myself should be disqualified. (ESV)

Living for Jesus amid the difficulties of life is no easy task. We all face trials, sorrows, losses, various types of abuse, and other afflictions along the way. In the hereafter, however, isn't it encouraging to know Jesus will recognize our endurance during these storms by bestowing on us an "imperishable" crown like the ones athletes received after winning races in the ancient Olympic games?.

The Apostle Peter spoke about our faithfulness during trials glorifying the Lord because it represents our firm trust in Him despite our circumstances:

> In this you rejoice, though now for a little while, if necessary, you have been grieved by various trials, so that the tested genuineness of your faith—more precious than gold that perishes though it is tested by fire—may be found to result in praise and glory and honor at the revelation of Jesus Christ. (1 Peter 1:6–7, ESV)

Our steadfastness during times of affliction will not only result in a reward, but will also magnify the greatness of our Savior.

2. The Crown of Rejoicing: Paul wrote about another reward in 1 Thessalonians 2:19:

> For what is our hope, or joy, or crown of rejoicing? Are not even ye in the presence of our Lord Jesus Christ at his coming?

Because the context points to the Thessalonian saints, whom Paul initially evangelized, many equate this wreath with a reward for leading others to saving faith in the Savior.

Pastor and author David Jeremiah adds insight:

This is sometimes called the Soul Winner's Crown, but I suspect it isn't just reserved for those who actually lead another person to Christ. I think it will be shared by all those who play a role in bringing others to Christ. It's a team effort.[34]

This one isn't just for missionaries, those who start churches, or those who lead others to the Savior. It's for all who support missions in numerous ways or who somehow plant seeds of faith in the hearts of others.

3. The Crown of Glory: In 1 Peter 5:2–5, the apostle referred to a "crown of glory" the Lord will present to faithful shepherds of His Church. The context doesn't limit this crown to being given only to the elders who teach, but extends it to all who faithfully guide the saints via positions of leadership or who exercise oversight in some way.

Concerning this crown, Ed Hindson wrote:

It has been said there are many pastors but few shepherds. The church has many leaders, but too few servants who truly live out the calling required for the crown of glory.[35]

In these last days, many pastors seem more concerned with filling the sanctuary's seats than in truly guiding their flocks. In many large churches, the elders rule while small group leaders are the ones who shepherd the congregants, tenderly caring for and feeding the lambs Jesus places under their care by instructing them in the Word of God and warning them of perils and abundant deceptions of living in the last days before the Tribulation period. The Lord will reward these leaders' faithfulness with a crown of glory because, in these roles, they fit better with the "elders" the apostle described in 1 Peter 5:2–5.

4. The Crown of Righteousness: This crown relates specifically to those who eagerly await Jesus' appearing. In 2 Timothy 4:8, we read:

Henceforth there is laid up for me a crown of righteousness, which the Lord, the righteous judge, shall give me at that day: and not to me only, but unto all them also that love his appearing.

This reward points to the most telling difference among born-again believers today. Many of us await the Rapture with eager anticipation. We long for Jesus to catch us up in the air and take us home to glory. We pray for Him to come for us soon.

Those who ignore the signs of the times and the immanency of Jesus' return disqualify themselves for this crown. How many will lose out on it because they never hear about the joys ahead for them in the hereafter?

Of course, all believers will be righteous when they stand before the Lord. We wouldn't be there if this weren't true. The context, however, links this crown to an excited expectation of Jesus to appear at any moment, even if it never happens in one's lifetime.

5. The Crown of Life: James 1:12 refers to a "crown of life" the Lord will give to those who "love him." Of course, all believers possess eternal life now and will stand before the Lord dressed in His righteousness alone. This reward is not about who will live forever in Heaven, but rather about who will receive special recognition for walking with wisdom through assorted trials of earthly life.

Since this reward appears in the context of faithfully weathering life's storms, it seems quite similar to the "imperishable crown" of 1 Corinthians 9:24–25, where Paul compared the latter to persevering in an athletic contest or race. The crown James has in mind is for those who not only endure severe trials with which the Lord tests their faith, but for those who emerge from those times with a great love for the Lord. Our salvation never for one moment rests on our affection for the Savior, but on His passion for us. It's quite another thing to say that, as saints, He will reward our love for Him that remains intact after times of affliction.

FOR HIS GLORY

Revelation 4:10 says we will "cast our crowns" before God's throne. In the next verse, we read that the twenty-four elders who represent the Body of Christ in Heaven are giving glory to the Lord for all things.

The rewards we receive will matter, and, as stated earlier, will determine our place of service in Jesus' thousand-year reign over the nations. At the same time, we will recognize His role in all we accomplish and give Him all the glory. We will realize that Jesus is the sole reason for our receipt of rewards and, in the end, all belong to Him.

QUALITY OVER QUANTITY

When it comes to rewards, we must resist the tendency to compare ourselves to others. We all have a unique mixture of spiritual gifts, talents, personalities, and opportunities. We mustn't look at Billy Graham and think of all the ways our own service to the Lord doesn't yield the type of results his ministry produced.

The words of Romans 12:3–8 provide great encouragement in this regard. In that passage, Paul described some of the gifts of the Holy Spirit and encouraged us to excel according to the ones we're given. The Lord provides differing measures of faith, spiritual abilities, and grace to fulfill His purposes for each of us. He will reward us for our faithfulness to use *what He endows to us* rather than what He gives those who preach, who evangelize multitudes, or even who is seated beside us at church.

In his book *Future Glory*, Ed Hindson quotes Erwin W. Lutzer, speaker, author, and former pastor of Moody Church in Chicago, in regard to our rewards:

> We do not know everything we would like to know about rewards. We simply do not understand how Christ will balance

our good deeds with those that are worthless. We must be content to know that Christ will be fair and generous. Whatever He does will be acceptable; no one will question His judgment. He will meticulously separate the perishable from the imperishable.[36]

Lutzer's words aptly sum up our discussion on rewards. There's much we don't know, but we can trust our Savior's tender love as we contemplate His examination of our lives and service for Him. We can also take great comfort in knowing the majority of our time in Heaven before the Second Coming will be filled with celebration, worship, and praise for our Lord. Regardless of the outcome at the *bema* seat, all the redeemed will take part in the marriage supper of the Lamb, a lengthy time of feasting and great jubilation.

Chapter 7

A Wedding and
Jubilant Celebration

Whether we live till Christ comes again, or whether we fall asleep
in him, many of us know that we shall sit down at the great
wedding feast in the end of the days, and we shall partake of
the supper of the Lamb in the day of his joy and glory. We are
looking across the blackness and darkness of the centuries into
that promised millennial age wherein we shall rejoice with our
Lord with joy unspeakable and full of glory.
~Charles Spurgeon, "Marriage Supper of the Lamb" sermon

The last book in the Bible begins with these words: "The revelation
of Jesus Christ." From beginning to end, the prophetic account
magnifies our Lord Jesus Christ. It's all about His glory, sovereignty, and
power. (See appendix C for how Revelation exalts our Savior.)

Within the pages of the Revelation, we catch glimpses of a jubilant
celebration in Heaven because of a wedding. In Ephesians 5:29–33, Paul
explained that the marriage between a man and a woman represents the
relationship of Jesus to His Church. Believers are not only the Body of
Christ, but we are also His Bride, a relationship the apostle described as

"a great mystery" (Ephesians 5:32). In the New Testament, a "mystery" represents something new, a subject or concept the Lord did not reveal in the Old Testament. It's also something we couldn't discover apart from God illuminating for us.

In 2 Corinthians 11:2, Paul wrote:

> For I feel a divine jealousy for you, since I betrothed you to one husband, to present you as a pure virgin to Christ. (ESV)

For the Church, this happened in the Upper Room with the disciples representing all future New Testament saints. In Jewish weddings of the first century, the betrothal happened about a year before the wedding. For us, the marriage of Jesus to His Church remains a future event.

As Christ's betrothed, we are inseparably and forever bound to Him. During the seven years of Tribulation on earth, the Church will formally become His Bride. We read about a wedding ceremony in Revelation 19:7:

> Let us be glad and rejoice, and give honor to him: for the marriage of the Lamb is come, and his wife hath made herself ready.

The joy we will feel at our wedding in Heaven will far exceed any happiness we've felt on earth, even at our own weddings.

The formal wedding announcement in Heaven comes after a time of thunderous praise for the Lord. The whole passage, Revelation 19:1–10, displays a time of great jubilation that even includes the angelic host. Some of the words of George Frideric Handel's "Hallelujah Chorus" come from Revelation 19:6:

> And I heard as it were the voice of a great multitude, and as the voice of many waters, and as the voice of mighty thundering, saying, Hallelujah: for the Lord God omnipotent reigneth.

We will all sing these words in one loud "voice" announcing Jesus' millennial rule over the nations. If you get goosebumps now from singing the "Hallelujah Chorus," just wait until the day we take part in the jubilant worship described in the opening verses of Revelation 19, when all of Heaven roars in loud, triumphant adoration of our King.

The Wedding

Many of us have fond memories of attending marriage ceremonies and receptions. As splendid as those occasions may have been, in Jesus' day, weddings were an even bigger deal. Can you imagine a celebration lasting many weeks or even longer? Hindson wrote the following about first-century wedding feasts:

> Jewish weddings included much more fanfare in first-century Jewish culture. A wedding could last an entire week, included large family gatherings, and impacted the entire community. In John 2, we see a picture of this when Jesus performed His first miracle at a wedding. His very presence at the wedding in Cana at the beginning of His ministry forecast the wedding in heaven that will come when the bride of Christ is taken up into the Father's house.[37]

For all of us, there's wonder and comfort in viewing the Church as the Bride of Christ. Jesus, as the loving Groom, will not fail to carry out any of His promises. Paul assured of this in Ephesians 5:25–27:

> Husbands, love your wives, even as Christ also loved the church, and gave himself for it; That he might sanctify and cleanse it with the washing of water by the word, That he might present it to himself a glorious church, not having spot, or wrinkle, or any such thing; but that it should be holy and without blemish.

We will "be holy and without blemish" when we stand before the Lord in Heaven. At the moment, we rest in Christ's righteousness given to us at the moment of salvation (see 2 Corinthians 5:21). That's the sole basis of our receiving eternal life. Apart from Jesus' perfect and sinless life and shed blood on the cross, we would have no hope of Heaven, let alone any prospects of celebrating a wedding once we arrive on the brighter shore.

We read about the completion of Jesus' redeeming work on behalf of His Bride in the following:

It was granted her to clothe herself with fine linen, bright and pure—for the fine linen is the righteous deeds of the saints. (Revelation 19:8, ESV)

Pastor and Bible commentator John MacArthur wrote the following about our adornment in future righteousness in preparation for the wedding as pictured in the above verse:

The fine linen with which the bride is clothed in the vision represents the righteous acts of the saints. At salvation, believers were clothed with Christ's righteousness, imputed to them.... But now the church is clothed with a righteousness of its own; the glorified believers are intrinsically righteous, like the holy angels. No longer will the church have only an imputed righteousness, but also then an imparted holy perfection.[38]

As MacArthur points out, as believers, we will one day appear before the Father dressed in Jesus' righteousness alone. The bright white robes we will wear in Heaven will display our blameless standing in God's sight.

Even though our good works result solely from the Lord's grace, along with His equipping power working through us, He will graciously adorn us with "fine linen" representing our virtuous deeds. Amazing! This is the height of mercy. Not one believer will deserve such glowing recognition, but Jesus will graciously honor all His saints in such a way. Is it any wonder our praise for Him will sound like thunder in Heaven?

The Wedding Feast

Now we come to part of a wedding celebration that most of us here on earth really look forward to: the reception, which inevitably involves delicious food—whether it's wedding cake and punch or a full meal. In Revelation 19:9, the angel speaking to John says, "Blessed are they which are called unto the marriage supper of the Lamb."

This feast will last a lot longer than those held during the typical week-long Jewish weddings of the first century; some commentators suggest we will participate in this event during much of our time in Heaven between the Rapture and the Second Coming. Not only will many of our loved ones from earth be with us, but we also might strike up conversations with apostles such as Paul or John. What might Matthew say about the day Jesus called him away from his tax collecting? What questions might we have for our loved ones who have who entered Heaven long before us? And, of course, Jesus not only will be our host, but also, He'll be by far the most honored presence in attendance. Imagine the questions we might ask Him (providing we don't forget amid the excitement of the feast!)?

Several excellent expositors of Scripture believe the marriage supper of the Lamb will take place on earth *after* the Second Coming. They include the Tribulation saints and redeemed Jews who survive the Day of the Lord as guests at the feast.

We (Terry and Jonathan), however, believe the great event will happen in Heaven *before* Jesus returns to earth. We agree that much feasting will take place during Jesus' millennial reign as pictured in Isaiah 25:6–9, but we place the marriage supper of the Lamb in glory ahead of the Second Coming.

Dr. Renald E. Showers, well-known theologian, speaker, author, and retired servant of the Lord with The Friends of Israel Gospel Ministry, wrote that the Jewish marriage customs of the first century AD support placing the supper in Heaven while the Tribulation rages on the earth:

In light of what has been seen [Jewish wedding customs], the following conclusions can be drawn concerning the relationship of the three steps of Jewish marriage customs to the marriage of Christ and the Church. First, the betrothal of Christ and the Church is taking place during the present Church age as people trust Jesus Christ to be their Savior (2 Cor. 11:2). Second, in the future Christ will take His bride, the Church, from this world to His Father's house in Heaven when He comes to rapture it (Jn. 14:2–3; 1 Th. 4:13–18). This will be the "marriage of the Lamb." Third, after the Rapture of the Church, the "marriage supper of the Lamb" will take place with the wedding guests who will have already been called and assembled.[39]

Regardless of when the celebratory feast occurs, we will all revel in its joy. In Psalm 16:11, we read David's words:

You make known to me the path of life; in your presence there is fullness of joy; at your right hand are pleasures forevermore.

When the events described in Revelation 19:1–10 arrive, our joy will know no bounds. Our happiest moments in this life will pale by comparison with that period.

Former pastor and current blogger Grant Phillips' words especially encapsulate the exuberance of this passage:

Every pulpit in this country should be proclaiming that Jesus is coming soon to remove His bride and then bring judgment upon a sin-depraved world. Instead, only a few eagerly await His return. Only a few have their nose pressed against the window, eagerly looking for the bridegroom.[40]

Sadly, the silence in many churches regarding what Scripture says about the hereafter deprives many saints of the excitement and joy they would feel in anticipation of Heaven. Instead, their focus remains earth-bound, disconnected from the hope firmly embedded in the Gospel message. Many pastors preach excellent sermons that speak to many needs, but they often fail to connect the wonders of Paradise to those starved for such hope in their congregations.

Words from Charles Spurgeon's sermon, "The Marriage Supper of the Lamb," reflect our happy celebration when we share this feast with our Savior:

> There will come a time when all God's redeemed shall be saved. There will come a day when all who have died shall have been raised again from the tomb, and those who remain alive shall have been changed, so that their corruption shall have put on incorruption, and mortality shall have put on immortality. *Then will the Church be perfect and complete;* no one member will be missing. There will be no spot or wrinkle remaining in her. Then it shall come to pass that Christ will celebrate this marriage supper, which will be the *bringing of the people of God into the closest and happiest union with Christ their Lord in glory.* Even now, the Lord Jesus Christ is no stranger to some of us, and we are not strangers to him; yet there shall come a day when we shall see him face to face, and then we shall know him with a clearer and fuller knowledge than is possible to us today. What

that bliss will be, I cannot tell. Oh, the ineffable brightness when we shall see the face of Jesus! Oh, the unspeakable sweetness when we shall hear his voice! Oh, the amazing bliss when he shall manifest himself to us in all his glory! And there will come such a day for all whom he has redeemed, for all who trust him, and rest in his atoning sacrifice. *That will be the marriage supper of the Lamb.*[41] (Italics in original)

Jesus will bring all New Testament saints to Heaven at the time of the Rapture; we will all participate in the wedding ceremony and the supper that will follow. Christ's perfect Bride, the Church, will be dressed in our Savior's righteousness and thus forever free from sin and its consequences.

Chapter 8

JOY TO THE WORLD—AND TO US!

This [Matthew 24:29–31] is the most prophesied event in the
Bible. The Old Testament contains many references to it. Some
Bible scholars estimate that one-tenth of all the verses in the
New Testament refer to this event, the coming of Jesus Christ
at the close of history. If all the references to Christ's return
were removed, the New Testament would become virtually
unintelligible. So the event we are about to examine is clearly one
of the most important occurrences in all of history.[42]

~RAY C. STEDMAN, *What on Earth Is Happening?*

Whenever we hear or sing "Joy to the World!" during the Christmas season, many of us think of Jesus' Second Coming. Isaac
Watts, however, intended for us to sing his lyrics when we remember the
Savior's birth; he based them on Psalm 98, which he believed predicted
the first advent:

"Joy to the World!" is Isaac Watts' interpretation of Psalm 98,
which says: "Shout joyfully to the Lord, all the earth" (verse 4).
As he read Psalm 98, Isaac pondered the real reason for shouting
joyfully to the Lord—the Messiah has come to redeem us.[43]

Of course, we rejoice because of Jesus' saving work on the cross and His resurrection during His initial time in this world. It's the basis of our hope in a fallen planet and a cause for glee during the Christmas season.

However, the account of the Lord's arrival in Psalm 98 relates to His Second Coming, not to His First. That passage is one of many Messianic Psalms that describes Christ's return to earth at the end of the Tribulation. It says the Messiah is coming to "judge the earth" (v. 9), which was not Jesus' mission during His first appearance, as He Himself clearly said:

I came not to judge the world, but to save the world. (John 12:47)

In the ancient world, kings served as both ruler and judge. They were the highest court in the land; they were the sole members of the nation's supreme court. When the psalmist said the Lord will "judge the world, and the people with equity" (Psalm 98:9), it's the same as saying He will reign over the nations of the earth as their King, because it defines one of His chief duties as the ruler.

Psalm 97 begins with these words that point to Jesus' return to earth:

The Lord reigns, let the earth rejoice; let the many coastlands be glad! (ESV)

The theme of rejoicing in Psalms 93–100 comes from the Lord's Second Coming, after which He will rule over the nations of the world. *That's the reason for rejoicing in these Messianic passages of Scripture. Please don't spiritualize these wonderful prophecies of Jesus' coming reign over earth.*

We also catch a glimpse of the boundless joy Jesus will bring to the world when He comes to rule in Psalm 96:11–13:

Let the heavens be glad, and let the earth rejoice; let the sea roar, and all that fills it; let the field exult, and everything in it! Then shall all the trees of the forest sing for joy before the Lord, for he comes, for he comes to judge the earth. He will judge the world in righteousness, and the peoples in his faithfulness. (ESV)

The first stanza of "Joy to the World" concludes by repeating the words, "And heaven and nature sing." Those words fit what Psalm 96 says about Jesus' return after the time of devastation during the Tribulation. Paul may have had this passage in mind when he wrote Romans 8:19:

For the creation waits with eager longing for the revealing of the sons of God. (ESV)

At the beginning of the second verse of "Joy to the World," Watts wrote, "Joy to the world! The Savior reigns." The fourth verse adds: "He rules the world with truth and grace." These words depict a future reality, the thousand-year reign of Jesus as described in Revelation 20:1–10. The choruses we cheerfully sing at Christmas don't align with current reality; Jesus doesn't yet rule over the nations of the world, as Psalm 99:1–2 proclaims:

The Lord reigns; let the peoples tremble! He sits enthroned upon the cherubim; let the earth quake! The Lord is great in Zion; he is exalted over all the peoples. (ESV)

The Messianic Psalms fit all the Bible says about Christ's Second Coming. It's then He will be "great in Zion" and "exalted over all the peoples," but not before.

THE GREAT CONTRAST

During the Christmas season, manger scenes are displayed in churches and in many homes. We couldn't write a script with a humbler beginning for anyone than what's recorded about the Savior's birth in Luke 2:1–21. The only people God told about His Son's arrival were lowly shepherds, the most despised group of that day. After seeing the angels and hearing them proclaim Jesus' birth, they rushed to Bethlehem.

The wise men arrived a year or two later from ancient Persia, where the prophet Daniel had once lived. It's likely they went to honor Jesus as a king based on the prophecies of Daniel from the book he wrote and possibly other writings he left behind.

If one word sums up Jesus' initial appearance in the world, it would be "humble." The purpose of His First Coming was "not to be served but to serve, and to give his life as a ransom for many" (Mark 10:45, ESV).

His Second Coming will be far different, to say the least. In fact, no single word can adequately describe His glorious return, although terms like "triumph," "power," and "spectacular" might be a good place to start. In Revelation 19:11–16, we read words that, in contrast to Jesus' lowly birth in Bethlehem, depict a majestic procession the likes of which the world has never before witnessed:

And I saw heaven opened, and behold a white horse; and he that sat upon him was called Faithful and True, and in righteousness he doth judge and make war. His eyes were as a flame of fire, and on his head were many crowns; and he had a name written, that no man knew, but he himself. And he was clothed with a vesture dipped in blood: and his name is called The Word of God. And the armies which were in heaven followed him upon white horses, clothed in fine linen, white and clean. And out of his mouth goeth a sharp sword, that with it he should smite the nations: and he shall rule them with a rod of iron: and he treadeth the winepress of the fierceness and wrath of Almighty God. And he hath on his vesture and on his thigh a name written, King Of Kings, and Lord Of Lords.

Ed Hindson beautifully describes these verses:

The singular vignette of Christ's return in Revelation 19:11–16 is the most dramatic passage in the entire Bible. In these six verses we are swept up into the triumphant entourage of redeemed saints as they ride in the heavenly procession with the King of kings and Lord of lords. In this one passage alone, all the hopes and dreams of every believer are finally and fully realized. This is not the Palm Sunday procession with the humble Messiah on the donkey colt. This is the ultimate in eschatological drama. The rejected Savior returns in triumph as the rightful King of the world—*and we are with him.*[44]

Hallelujah!

Jesus' return to earth will mark the grand finale of human history and the inauguration of the greatest kingdom the world will have ever seen. Try to imagine what those who are alive at that time will see. Revelation 19:11–16 provides the perspective from Heaven; Jesus tells us what those dwelling on earth will see as He majestically rides across the sky:

Immediately after the tribulation of those days shall the sun be darkened, and the moon shall not give her light, and the stars shall fall from heaven, and the powers of the heavens shall be shaken: And then shall appear the sign of the Son of man in heaven: and then shall all the tribes of the earth mourn, and they shall see the Son of man coming in the clouds of heaven with power and great glory. (Matthew 24–30).

By the end of the Tribulation, a substantial number of people from the nations of the world will have taken the mark of the Beast and survived the judgments of the Day of the Lord. They are the ones who will mourn at the sight of Jesus returning, because they will know that His arrival seals their eternal doom.

The armies gathered against Zion to fight the battle we know as Armageddon will also tremble with fear at the sight. Once they see Jesus with the vast armies of Heaven behind Him, they'll realize their demise is near. Their destruction will come quickly; they won't even have the opportunity to fight against the Lord.

For the earthbound Gentiles who, through a remarkable demonstration of their strong faith, will have refused to take the mark of the Beast of the beast and *somehow* managed to remain alive during the worst time in history, the sight of Jesus on a white horse will bring great relief. They will celebrate the coming defeat of the one preoccupied with killing them. Christ's appearance will mean life rather than their certain death.

The last half of the Tribulation will be a nightmare for the Jewish people. Antichrist will kill a great many, with only one-third surviving his deadly rampage (Zechariah 13:7–9). Those who remain will weep tears of repentance as they realize their ancestors killed their Messiah (Zechariah 12:10–13:1). However, their tears of sorrow will gradually turn to ones of joy as they watch the Lord return with the promise of a restored kingdom. They will watch as He later takes His rightful place on the throne of David (Isaiah 9:6–7).

At His Second Coming, those in Israel will fulfill Jesus' prophetic words recorded in Matthew 23:39:

For I say unto you, Ye shall not see me henceforth, till ye shall say, Blessed is he that cometh in the name of the Lord.

The result will be far different than what happened after the Savior heard these words upon his entry into Jerusalem during the time we remember on Palm Sunday (Matthew 20:6). The people later rejected Him and called for His crucifixion. However, as stated in the above verse, the Lord looked forward to the day when all of Israel would say these words and anoint Him as their King. This awaits a future fulfillment; Israel has yet to carry out what Jesus prophesied in Matthew 23:39.

THROUGH THE SKY

Jesus' triumphant return to earth is a key part of our hereafter. This isn't a tale of what will happen to other people; it's something all those who have trusted Christ for salvation will experience firsthand. All the saints from the Day of Pentecost to the time of the Rapture will be with the Lord when He returns, clothed in white garments. *What an amazing sight that will be!*

Thomas Boston, an early eighteenth-century church leader and theologian, wrote the following about the significance of the robes the Lord will give us during our time Heaven at the *bema* seat of Christ. We will wear these robes as we ride back to earth with Him:

> The Romans, when they set their bond-servants free, gave them a white garment as a badge of their freedom. So shall the saints that day receive their white robes; for it is the day of "the glorious liberty of the children of God" (Rom. 8:21)....
>
> White raiment was a token of purity. Therefore the Lamb's wife is "arrayed in fine linen, clean and white" (Rev. 19:8).... The saints shall then put on robes of perfect purity, and shine in spotless holiness. Absolute innocence shall then be restored, and every appearance of sin banished far from this kingdom.[45]

Ephesians 1:4 states we are "holy and without blame before him in love." On that day, this reality will be our experience. We will be forever free from the presence of sin, as signified by our "fine linen, clean and white."

The eyes of the world will be on Jesus, and on us, as we ride with Him through the sky toward Jerusalem. It's impossible to capture in words the excitement we will feel at that moment. Can we even picture the scene of riding through the air on horses with glorified and immortal bodies?

Imagine what you might be thinking on that day. What feelings might well up inside you? What name will you give your white horse? This isn't bland theology with no relevance to us; we will be with Jesus and share in His ultimate victory over the dark forces of this world.

While Christ was hanging on the cross, many thoughts might have raced across His mind as He looked to the joy ahead (Hebrews 12:2). It seems probable that His victorious return with us, His Bride, was one of those thoughts.

WHY IS JESUS' SECOND COMING SIGNIFICANT?

Besides the fact that we as the redeemed will participate in the Second Coming, are there other reasons for us to look forward to it? Absolutely! Here are a few:

1. The Second Coming is the most anticipated event of Scripture. The Old Testament includes about three hundred prophetic references to Christ's First Advent. However, according to Grant Jeffrey, a leading Bible prophecy teacher, the Scriptures contain eight times that number of verses that speak of Jesus' return to earth.[46] Since God's Word emphasizes this event to such an extent, shouldn't it be something we anticipate as well?

Enoch spoke of the Second Coming even long before the Flood of Noah's time:

> And Enoch also, the seventh from Adam, prophesied of these, saying, Behold, the Lord cometh with ten thousands of his saints, to execute judgment upon all, and to convince all that are ungodly among them of all their ungodly deeds which they have ungodly committed, and of all their hard speeches which ungodly sinners have spoken against him. (Jude 14–15)

If Jesus' return to earth was on God's mind that long ago, doesn't that carry a great deal of significance? Of course! Enoch didn't generate this revelation on his own; God revealed it to the patriarch during the times he had walked with Him so very long ago. Thousands of years before His crucifixion, the Lord was already thinking of the day He would return to the world with power and majesty to rule over the nations.

Don't let anyone deceive you by claiming the Second Coming happened in AD 70. How can anyone claim that something so marvelous and history-changing happened with such miniscule fanfare in the first century AD when Titus attacked Jerusalem?

2. The Second Coming marks Jesus' return to Jerusalem. After destroying the kingdom of Antichrist and sending him and the False Prophet into the flames of Hell, Jesus will set His feet down in the land of Israel where He walked during his time on earth. In Zechariah 14:3–4, we read:

> Then shall the LORD go forth, and fight against those nations, as when he fought in the day of battle. And his feet shall stand in that day upon the mount of Olives, which is before Jerusalem on the east, and the mount of Olives shall cleave in the midst thereof toward the east and toward the west, and there shall be a

very great valley; and half of the mountain shall remove toward the north, and half of it toward the south.

Just as Jesus predicted in Matthew 23:39, He will return to the city that once rejected Him and receive a welcome fitting for a King, the Messiah.

3. During His return, Jesus completes the destruction of Satan's kingdom, headed up by Antichrist. Today, we see evil and lawlessness growing exponentially as the world rapidly moves toward a tyrannical, one-world government. As never before, the pieces are coming together for the implementation of the mark of the Beast John described in Revelation 13:16–18. As never before in history, the technology and plans exist for Antichrist to control commerce throughout the world.

We're tempted to despair as wickedness, deceit, and lawlessness gain the upper hand all around us. The Second Coming, however, assures us that the scheming of the elite globalists will be all for nothing. Their plans will succeed for a brief time, but Christ will destroy both Antichrist and his kingdom when He returns. The words of Psalm 37:1–20 help us understand and believe what we cannot see. The Lord will surely judge the wicked during the Tribulation and then complete their demise at the time of His return.

4. The words of Psalm 46:10 find their fulfillment with Jesus' return:

Be still, and know that I am God: I will be exalted among the heathen, I will be exalted in the earth.

We can remain calm in the midst of perilous times because God sovereignly controls history. We will see the day when all the nations that now despise Jesus will exalt Him and recognize His deity. That alone is enough to bring a big smile to our faces!

5. Jesus' victorious ride back to earth assures us of an eternity of bliss. Despite the many ups and downs of this life; we know that surpassing joy and glory await us upon its conclusion.

In Jonathan's book, *The Triumph of the Redeemed*, he wrote:

> We don't know where life will take us. We can be certain, however, that Jesus loves us more than we can understand and will not fail to safely bring us to His eternal kingdom. Jesus' power, as displayed at His Second Coming, assures us that nothing is impossible with Him. He is able to keep all His promises of a future life that will exceed all of our expectations. The promise of Revelation 21:4 will be ours for all eternity.
>
> Life can be cruel and difficult; at times we all feel like throwing up our hands as we exclaim, "What's the use!?" However, this current existence is not the end of our story. Regardless of our current afflictions, we look forward to the time when we will share in Jesus' triumph over Satan and the nations that once rejected Him (and continue to do so).[47]

Oh, what joy that day will bring. We can sing "Joy to the World" all year long as a reminder of the over-the-top bliss ahead for all those of us who have placed our faith and hope securely in Christ. The hymn, "Joyful, Joyful, We Adore Thee" also comes to mind. Something similar to these might be our forever song to the Lord.

Chapter 9

WE WILL INHERIT A KINGDOM

The idea of *futurity* is also present in a number of passages which speak of the Kingdom as something which members of the *ekklesia* [the church] shall inherit (1 Cor. 6:9, 10; 15:50; Gal. 5:21; Eph. 5:5; Jas. 2:5). The Apostle Paul not only sees this inheritance of a kingdom in a future time but definitely excludes it from the present age by placing it after the resurrection and rapture of the church.[48]

~ALVA J. MCCLAIN, *The Greatness of the Kingdom*

I n Revelation 20:1–10, John unveiled a thousand-year period of time referred to as the Millennium, during which Christ will reign over the nations of the earth. This isn't the eternal state, as those who enter this millennial kingdom will sin, as exemplified by the rebellion against Christ at the end of this period.

This is referred to as Jesus' premillennial return to Earth, which simply means the Second Coming will take place between the seven-year Tribulation and the start of Jesus' thousand-year reign on the throne of David. For most of the twentieth century, the majority of Bible-believing churches in America and in other parts of the world adhered to this belief.

Since the year 2000, however, replacement theology in its various forms has taken up residence in many churches. Contrary to what Scripture teaches, this doctrine asserts that God rejected Israel after Jesus' crucifixion and He applied His promise of a future kingdom to the Church. A variant form of amillennialism (the belief that there is no Millennium), states Jesus fulfilled all the covenants with and promises to the Israelites at His First Coming. Both teachings eliminate Jesus' physical kingdom based in Jerusalem as prophesied in the Old Testament and equate the period described in Revelation 20:1–10 with either the Church Age or the eternal state.

Why bring up the matter of errant teaching? Why is it important to understand that Jesus will reign from a restored kingdom to Israel? The answer is because the spiritualization of Jesus' earthly kingdom clouds the reality of our experience in the hereafter and erodes the splendor of Jesus' return. Those who transfer the kingdom promises to the Church in such a way erase the biblical anticipation of Jesus' appearing for His Church and keep us on earth as spectators rather than participants in the great event.

Grant Jeffrey, said the following about the importance of recognizing Jesus' future return as King:

> If we are to understand the hundreds of specific prophecies about the divine plan of God to establish His kingdom on earth, we must first attempt to understand the fundamental biblical truth regarding the Second Coming and its relation to the time of the coming Millennium.[49]

As we will see, the millennial kingdom is our inheritance as New Testament saints. The Lord has promised us roles of service to perform in this realm. Those who equate this with the Church greatly err and vastly diminish the significance of our becoming coheirs with Christ.

The near-term fallout of equating the Church to God's promise of a kingdom to Israel is that of two popular false teachings that have taken hold of many churches and have further darkened the biblical picture of eternity.

The first errant teaching is dominion theology, or the New Apostolic Reformation (NAR). Those who hold to this belief say the Church will convert the world to Christ and bring in a righteous rule upon the earth *before* Jesus returns. In other words, members of the Church—rather than Jesus—will rule during the Millennium. They believe the Church will soon rise up victorious over the evil forces gaining control of the world.

Dominion theology/NAR adherents believe the Lord has raised up new apostles and prophets today to proclaim His new revelation to us. Although it's the most popular of the errant beliefs regarding the end times, dominion theology thoroughly contradicts what Scripture says about the topic. The Bible *never* states that the Church will triumph over wickedness in the world, nor does it assign such kingdom responsibilities to the Body of Christ. God's Word says the Lord will return to earth before the Millennium.

Furthermore, this false teaching makes the Millennium meaningless for those who have already died as followers of Christ and renders it terribly bland compared to what the Bible teaches.

The second grievous error asserts that Jesus returned to the earth in AD 70, and at that time fulfilled most, if not all, of future Bible prophecy. The extreme preterists assert that we are already in the eternal state. The milder and more prevalent form of this heresy still looks forward to the eternal state, but regards most other prophecies as having already been fulfilled. This teaching in all its forms is blatantly unbiblical.

Both of these teachings, all of which begin with the amillennial viewpoint of spiritualizing God's promises to Israel, glorify the Church rather than Jesus and paint a far less captivating picture of eternity than the one described in God's Word.

The Bible teaches that Jesus' thousand-year kingdom will be physical, and we will reign with Him.

PREMILLENNIALISM IN THE EARLY CHURCH

Premillennialism is not just a concept that flourished during the late nineteenth and twentieth centuries, it was the predominant belief during the early centuries of the Church.

Scripture alone must be our sole source of beliefs. A brief look at the early years of the Church establishes premillennialism as the prevailing belief during that time. While not all in the early Church agreed on the future of Israel, they nonetheless believed that what the Apostle John wrote in Revelation 20:1–10 regarding a thousand-year span between the Tribulation and eternity when Jesus would rule over the nations of the earth.

Justin Martyr (AD 100–165)

Justin Martyr, in his famous book, *Dialogue with Trypho*, affirmed "the premillennial return of Christ and the resurrection of the righteous before the beginning of the thousand-year kingdom."[50]

Below are his words concerning the Millennium:

But I and others, who are right-minded Christians on all points, are assured that there will be a resurrection of the dead, and a thousand years in Jerusalem, which will be built, adorned, and enlarged, [as] the prophets Ezekiel and Isaiah declare.... And further, there was a certain man with us, whose name was John, one of the apostles of Christ, who prophesied, by a revelation that was made to him, that those who believed in our Christ would dwell a thousand years in Jerusalem.[51]

Unfortunately, Martyr taught that God had rejected Israel, but it did not result in the amillennial views popular today. The above words show he believed Jesus would reign over the earth from the city of Jerusalem for a thousand years.

The premillennialism that dominated the early centuries of the Church was not the dispensationalism of today; neither was it what many refer to as "historic premillennialism," which denies the literalness of Jesus' thousand-year reign. Until the time of Augustine in the fifth century, the prevailing viewpoint in the Church was that Jesus would literally fulfill the words of Revelation 20:1–10.

Irenaeus (AD 130–202)

Irenaeus, a prominent early Church leader and theologian, wrote the following in AD 180 in his book, *Against Heresies* (book 5, chapter 30):

> But when this Antichrist shall have devastated all things in this world, he will reign for three years and six months, and sit in the temple at Jerusalem; and then the Lord will come from heaven in the clouds, in the glory of the Father, sending this man and those who follow him into the lake of fire; but bringing in for the righteous the times of the kingdom, that is, the hallowed seventh day; and restoring to Abraham the promised inheritance, in which kingdom the Lord declared, that "many coming from the east and from the west should sit down with Abraham, Isaac, and Jacob."[52]

This highly respected theologian wrote about things such as Antichrist, the Tribulation, and the Second Coming in a way that affirms interpreting the book of Revelation as a record of future prophecy rather than as allegory or something with no meaning to the Church today.

The ancient town of Smyrna was one of the original seven destinations of the letters John wrote from the isle of Patmos, as recorded in the book of Revelation. Polycarp, a disciple of the apostle, would've been the head of the Church gatherings in the town. Years later, Polycarp mentored Irenaeus in the faith before he left to become bishop in Lyons, France.

Why do we mention this? Irenaeus' literal interpretation of the book of Revelation came from Polycarp, who not only was a disciple of John, but was one of the first to see the book after the apostle wrote it. The fact that he passed on such a view of John's writings is more than a little significant.

Tertullian (AD 155–240)

We will conclude our brief look at premillennialism in the early Church with another highly visible and respected theologian, Tertullian, who resided in Carthage, a Roman province of Africa. He was also a prolific author and apologist, or defender of the faith. In his book, *Against Marcion*, he upheld "the literal reality of both the thousand-year kingdom of Christ on earth as well as the reality of the New Jerusalem."[53] He was just one of many early theologians in the Church who affirmed the millennial reign of Jesus as something distinct from the Church Age.

Those who guided believers in the early centuries of the Church believed Jesus would return as King and then rule over the nations. They did not spiritualize John's words in Revelation 20:1–10 to make them apply to the Church Age or eternal state, but they correctly saw them as referring to a distinct thousand-year rule of Christ.

HEIRS TO A GREAT KINGDOM

Beginning with King Nebuchadnezzar's dream, God revealed the progression of earthly kingdoms to the prophet Daniel, realms that would lead to Jesus' worldwide empire during the Millennium. Daniel's words regarding Greece and Rome were so specific and accurate that many critics claim he couldn't have written the book during the sixth century BC.

Daniel the prophet revealed what he saw regarding a *still-future realm*, the one over which Jesus will rule:

> I saw in the night visions, and, behold, one like the Son of man came with the clouds of heaven, and came to the Ancient of days, and they brought him near before him. And there was given him dominion, and glory, and a kingdom, that all people, nations, and languages, should serve him: his dominion is an everlasting dominion, which shall not pass away, and his kingdom that which shall not be destroyed. (Daniel 7:13–14)

The scene is in Heaven as the "Ancient of Days," God the Father, bestows a kingdom of Jesus, which includes "all people, nations, and languages," who will "serve him." In Matthew 26:64, the Lord claimed this prophecy for Himself, which resulted in a charge of blasphemy and a sentence of death by the Sanhedrin (Matthew 26:65–66).

Those who claim the Church is the new Israel change the direction of Jesus' movement in Matthew 26:64. They say that as Jesus was leaving the earth, He received the kingdom, which is now the Church. This contradicts Jesus' interpretation of Daniel 7:13–14 where the prophet said the Father would give Him the kingdom before He returned to the earth, not as He was leaving it.

Why is this distinction so important? Because the true kingdom of God is one we have yet to inherit along with the Lord. Daniel confirmed this futuristic timeline:

And the kingdom and dominion, and the greatness of the kingdom under the whole heaven, shall be given to the people of the saints of the most High, whose kingdom is an everlasting kingdom, and all dominions shall serve and obey him. (Daniel 7:27)

Two points in this passage are worth emphasizing. First, Jesus hasn't fulfilled the promises of Daniel 7; the night before He died on the cross, He was looking ahead to them. Second, "the saints of the most High," which includes us, will inherit the kingdom along with Jesus—which, according to verses 13–14, signifies that "all people, nations, and languages, should serve him." This will happen after the Second Coming; it's clearly an event set in the future.

The New Testament speaks of believers as "heirs"; specifically, Romans 8:17 refers to us as "joint heirs with Christ." Paul said "we have obtained an inheritance" with the Holy Spirit as the guarantee that we will someday receive it (Ephesians 1:11–14). All the New Testament verses that speak of our inheritance of a kingdom refer to it as something that will take place in the future.

Listen, my beloved brothers, has not God chosen those who are poor in the world to be rich in faith and heirs of the kingdom, which he has promised to those who love him? (James 2:5, ESV)

Our current status as members of the Body of Christ is that we are "heirs" of the kingdom, not "possessors" of it.
The Apostle Paul explained when we will inherit the kingdom:

Now this I say, brethren, that flesh and blood cannot inherit the kingdom of God; neither doth corruption inherit incorruption. Behold, I shew you a mystery; We shall not all sleep, but we shall all be changed. In a moment, in the twinkling of an eye, at the last trump: for the trumpet shall sound, and the dead shall be raised incorruptible, and we shall be changed. (1 Corinthians 15:50–52)

According to the apostle, we can't inherit the kingdom until after the Rapture, because it's impossible to do so in our flesh-and-blood bodies. Jesus will make us eligible for our inheritance by giving us imperishable bodies when He appears to take us to glory. In the meantime, the Holy Spirit is "the earnest of our inheritance;" the guarantee of our future possession of the kingdom (Ephesians 1:14).

In several other passages, Paul warned readers of behaviors that typify those who will not inherit God's kingdom (see 1 Corinthians 6:9, 10; 15:50; Galatians 5:21; Ephesians 5:5). His point is not that avoiding these things can earn us salvation, but that since they are characteristics of those who do not have a saving relationship with Christ, we should not behave like them. Only those who are redeemed by Jesus' blood are promised a kingdom.

In the next couple of chapters, we will examine Israel's place in the future realm and the mountain from which Jesus will reign. We may not understand all the implications, but they are critical aspects of our upcoming inheritance as New Testament saints.

BEYOND AMAZING

Jesus' thousand-year reign as King over the earth is central to the fulfillment of biblical prophecy. Words fail to adequately describe the excitement, the wonder, the delights, the splendor, and the rapturous joy we will feel when we begin to experience life in our immortal bodies. Our focus on such promises helps us deal with the many sorrows and afflictions of this life.

Jesus will return to earth as King. It's beyond amazing to consider that, as heirs, we will be part of His glorious kingdom; we will rule alongside our Savior. We will *inherit* a kingdom!

To again quote Ed Hindson, from his book *Future Glory*, the following sums up the remarkable prophecy of Jesus' thousand-year rule:

> One of the most incredible prophecies in the Bible is the coming of the kingdom of Christ to earth. Those of us who believe in the Rapture are often criticized for being escapists who want to abandon the planet God created. In reality, nothing could be further from the truth. We actually believe we are coming back to reign with Christ for one thousand years during His millennial kingdom.[54]

This is our hereafter, and it will indeed far exceed our most fanciful thoughts about it. The Bible tells us enough to fill us with great anticipation of this time.

On earth, the discovery that we are heirs to a million dollars when a rich uncle dies might cause much excitement. However, that's only a pittance compared to what it means to be coheirs with Jesus of a glorious kingdom. Can any amount of money compare with being a part of magnificent Kingdom that lasts for a thousand years and after that extends into eternity? No, especially considering the brevity of life compared with forever.

Chapter 10

ISRAEL'S RETURN TO GLORY

While it is true that the millennium (that is, one thousand years) is found only in Revelation 20, the belief in the Messianic kingdom does not rest on this passage alone. In fact, it hardly rests on it at all. The basis for the belief in the Messianic kingdom is twofold. First, there are the unfulfilled promises of the Jewish covenants, promises that can only be fulfilled in a Messianic kingdom. Second, there are the unfulfilled prophecies of the Hebrew Scriptures, prophecies speak of the coming of the Messiah who will reign on David's throne and rule over a peaceful kingdom. There is a great amount of material in the Hebrew Scriptures on the Messianic kingdom, and the belief in such a kingdom rests on the basis of a literal interpretation of this massive material.[55]

~DR. ARNOLD G. FRUCHTENBAUM, *The Footsteps of the Messiah*

In the previous chapter, we explored the millennial kingdom from the perspective that we are coheirs of it with Jesus. Now we will begin to describe this future realm over which we will rule alongside our Lord, which will include the restoration of a kingdom to Israel. Because this will play a major part in our future as coregents; it's also important that we understand why it's important in Bible prophecy.

First, the restoration of a kingdom to Israel upholds the integrity of God's Word. A multitude of prophecies predict Israel's revival as a nation. The way we explain these passages either enforces or diminishes the reliability of the entire Bible.

Second, the miraculous reemergence of Israel as a nation tells us we live in the last days before Jesus' appearing and the beginning of the Tribulation. The fulfillment of prophecy played a key role in Jesus' First Coming, and it has an even larger function in helping us understand the signs of the times in which we now live.

We believe Israel's existence as a nation in its ancient homeland, and with its ancient language, Hebrew, is a direct fulfillment of prophecy and a sign that we live in biblical times. We don't see how it can be otherwise. Israel has to be back in the land for the final prophecies to roll out as foretold. That's at the very heart of end-times events.

Third, our responsibilities as New Testament saints during the Millennium would be radically different apart from the restoration of Israel. Those who deny a future for Israel also deny Jesus' thousand-year reign as recorded in Revelation 20:1–10. The issue of a restoration of a kingdom for Israel makes a stark difference regarding what it means for us to inherit a kingdom.

Fourth, much of what we know about our lives in Jesus' future kingdom comes from Old Testament passages that assume the existence of a restored Israel. If we subtract its future as a nation from them, we lose much of our understanding of what it will mean to reign with the Lord.

A RESTORED KINGDOM

As Dr. Fruchtenbaum stated in the quote at the beginning of this chapter, a voluminous amount of Scripture points to the restoration of a glorious kingdom for Israel. Those who claim God has rejected Israel and replaced the nation with the Church must spiritualize hundreds, if not thousands, of verses to retrofit them into their viewpoint.

Do you see what a significant difference it makes for us as believers? If the Church now fulfills the Lord's kingdom promises to Israel, then we are now reigning with Christ and are already recipients of our promised inheritance. How disappointing! Thankfully, that's not what the Bible teaches; it says we will rule alongside Jesus in a *future* kingdom that includes a restored Israel—and we will do so with imperishable bodies. That's reassuring!

In order to fortify and explain our anticipation of ruling with Jesus in the Millennium, we'll present a brief defense of God's intention to restore a kingdom Israel.

Moments before Jesus ascended into Heaven, the disciples asked Him this question:

Lord, will you at this time restore the kingdom to Israel? (Acts 1:6)

The disciples, having received instruction in both prophecy (Luke 24:44–47) and the kingdom (Acts 1:3) after the Resurrection, remained confident of God's intention to fulfill His promises to Israel.

The Savior's response to His followers is key to our understanding:

It is not for you to know times or seasons that the Father has fixed by his own authority. (Acts 1:7)

Please note that, rather than altogether negating the disciples' assumption, Jesus told them their *timing* was wrong. The future restoration would happen, but it would occur at a time determined by the Father.

Jesus didn't squelch His disciples' expectations, but directed their attention to the task at hand: proclaiming the Gospel to a lost world (Acts 1:8).

The premise of the disciples' question about restoring a kingdom to Israel comes directly from Old Testament prophecies. The men might have had Jeremiah 30:1–3 in mind when they asked it:

> The word that came to Jeremiah from the LORD: "Thus says the LORD, the God of Israel: Write in a book all the words that I have spoken to you. For behold, days are coming, declares the LORD, when **I will restore the fortunes of my people, Israel and Judah**, says the LORD, and I will bring them back to the land that I gave to their fathers, and they shall take possession of it." (ESV, emphasis added)

This passage cannot apply to Judah's return from captivity in Babylon, because the prophecy includes both Israel and Judah. Such a combined kingdom hasn't existed since the early days of King Rehoboam, but will occur again in Jesus' kingdom.

Several other ancient prophets repeated the theme of a renewed kingdom for Israel. Zephaniah wrote the following:

> At that time I will bring you in, at the time when I gather you together; for I will make you renowned and praised among all the peoples of the earth, when I **restore your fortunes** before your eyes, says the Lord. (Zephaniah 3:20, ESV; emphasis added)

In Amos 9:14–15, the prophet repeats this familiar theme:

> I will **restore the fortunes of my people Israel**.... I will plant them on their land, and they shall never again be uprooted out of the land that I have given them. (Emphasis added, ESV)

Despite severe warnings of judgment for Judah, the prophet Joel concluded his book with strong reassurances for both Judah and Jerusalem:

So you shall know that I am the LORD your God, who dwells in Zion, my holy mountain. And Jerusalem shall be holy and strangers shall never again pass through it.... But Judah shall be inhabited forever, and Jerusalem to all generations. (Joel 3:17, 20, ESV)

The preceding verses couldn't state God's promises to Israel any clearer: "The Lord will *permanently bring* the people of Israel back to their land, something He hasn't yet done but will do in the future. What we see today is just the beginning of God's purposes for regathering His people."[56]

In Romans 11:2, Paul assured us that the words of Jeremiah still applied in his day:

God has not rejected his people whom he foreknew.

The realm over which we will reign alongside Jesus will include a gloriously restored Israel. As a result, we gain valuable insight into our future kingdom responsibilities by looking into its details.

THE SPECIFICS OF THE BLESSING

Ezekiel 36:22–38 gives us vivid picture of the Lord's future blessing of Israel. Although we see glimpses of what's to come in current-day Israel, the specifics await future fulfillment. The list below provides several details of what God will do in the future for His chosen people:

- He will gather them from the nations and bring them to their "own land" (v. 24).
- He will cleanse them from their sins and give them a new heart (vv. 25–26).

- He will put His Spirit within them (v. 27).
- They will never again experience a famine (vv. 29–30).
- The surrounding nations will recognize the supernatural aspect of Israel's restoration and glorify the Lord as a result (vv. 36, 38).

Besides those listed above, what other promises did the Lord make to Israel about the Millennium?

1. Abundant harvests rather than famine: In Ezekiel 36:29b–30, the Lord promised that Israel would never again experience a famine.

> And I will summon the grain and make it abundant and lay no famine upon you. I will make the fruit of the tree and the increase of the field abundant, that you may never again suffer the disgrace of famine among the nations. (ESV)

Later, in Ezekiel 36, the Lord quoted the people of this future day as saying:

> This land that was desolate has become like the garden of Eden, and the waste and desolate and ruined cities are now fortified and inhabited. (Ezekiel 36:35, ESV)

2. The rebuilding and inhabitation of ruined cities: In chapter 4, we examined the devastation that will come upon the world as the result of the wars and God's wrath during the Tribulation. One of the biggest battles during this time, Armageddon, will take place near Jerusalem as Satan makes one last attempt to stop Jesus from inheriting His kingdom. All these things will result in much destruction to the cities in Israel.

As a result, the ruined cities will need rebuilding, for which the Lord will claim all the credit:

Then the nations that are left all around you shall know that I am the Lord; I have rebuilt the ruined places and replanted that which was desolate. I am the Lord; I have spoken, and I will do it. (Ezekiel 36:36, ESV)

The Lord also promised to fill those cities with people (Ezekiel 36:37–38). Even though just a remnant of the Israelites will remain after the Tribulation, their number will grow rapidly during the time of unprecedented blessing during the Millennium. The Lord will add new cities besides the ones He rebuilds to deal with the population growth.

During this thousand-year period, Israel will finally possess all the land the Lord promised Abraham in Genesis 15:12–21. Even during the expanse of Israel's kingdom during the days of Kings David and Solomon, the nation never occupied all that God initially promised them. During the Millennium, however, they will.

3. Security: Many Old Testament prophets refer to the time when Jerusalem will dwell securely without the fear of war or destruction (Zephaniah 3:14–17; Zechariah 14:10–11).

In Ezekiel 37:24–28, the Lord promised to make a "covenant of peace" with His people. This pact, also mentioned in Isaiah 54:10, speaks of a future time of absolute security for Israel. The often-repeated phrase in Isaiah 54:17, "no weapon that is fashioned against you shall succeed," refers to the Jewish nation during the Millennium. It's the result of God's "covenant of peace."

In Isaiah 60, we find more far-reaching promises regarding the future peace Israel will enjoy during Jesus' reign. Note the assurance the Lord gives His people in verse 12:

For the nation and kingdom that will not serve thee shall perish; yea, those nations shall be utterly wasted.

Not only will this be a time of unprecedented safety for the Israelites, but other countries will also "serve" them. With Jesus ruling over all the earth from Jerusalem, who would even dare attack them?

4. Jesus will reign from Jerusalem: The Lord will rule over the nations from Jerusalem (see Zechariah 14:9–21). Many of the Psalms specify Zion, a location with the city, as the place of His throne (Psalm 97:8; 99:1–2). Although some of the early Church theologians such as Justin Martyr and Irenaeus dismissed the idea of Israel's restoration, they still maintained Jerusalem would be the place where Jesus would reign.

Jesus will someday sit on the throne of David (Isaiah 9:6–7; Luke 1:32–33). Where else could this be but in Jerusalem during the Millennium?

Chapter 11

A MOUNTAINTOP EXPERIENCE

At the time of the second coming of the Messiah, the land will undergo some tremendous geographical changes. One of the key transformations will be the rise of a mountain that will become the highest mountain in the world. On its summit will stand the Millennial Temple and the millennial Jerusalem.[57]

~DR. ARNOLD G. FRUCHTENBAUM, *The Footsteps of the Messiah*

During the Millennium, there will be a mountain we will often visit; we will also spend much time at its peak. It's a little-known aspect of Jesus' reign, but we will become quite familiar with its terrain.

In Ezekiel chapters 40–48, the prophet describes a temple located high on a mountain that's distinct from any other such structure that has ever existed or will appear during the Tribulation. Many dismiss this prophecy because they don't understand the vital role the temple will play in Israel's worship of the Lord during the kingdom. Prophecy speaker and author Ron Rhodes wrote:

The temple will be a worship center of Jesus Christ during the entire millennium. It will be built at the beginning of the messianic kingdom (Ezekiel 37:26–28) by Christ (Zechariah 6:12–13), redeemed Jews (Ezekiel 43:10–11), and representatives from the Gentile nations (Haggai 2:7; Zechariah 6:15).[58]

Ed Hindson, in *Future Glory*, said, "This final temple will exist in Jerusalem as the place where Christ is worshipped on earth."[59] He also wrote the following concerning this future Millennial Temple:

A full description of this temple and its courts is given in Ezekiel 40:1-44:31. No such building as Ezekiel so minutely describes has ever been built.... Since there is no temple in the New Jerusalem (Revelation 21:22), this must be a description of the temple that will be on earth during the millennium. That it does not belong to the new earth is also clear from Ezekiel's mention of seas and deserts and other locations that will not be found on the new earth after its renovation by fire.[60]

We shouldn't dismiss Ezekiel's vision of a future temple, as many do, just because we don't understand its purpose. If we rely just on our own reasoning, the idea of the Rapture interrupting life in this world followed by a lengthy time of God's wrath on the earth and Jesus' reign over the nations might also seem a bit far-fetched. However, we believe these things because God's Word says they will happen, and the Bible has a 100 percent accuracy record of fulfilled prophecies.

Likewise, we should view what Ezekiel says about this future place of worship in the same way.

Although this prophecy might seem obscure, it's central to the kingdom we will inherit. Furthermore, this is the place the Lord identifies as the site of His throne when He rules over the nations.

A GLORIOUS PLACE FOR A THRONE

A most profound prophecy is the fact that the Messiah—the returning Lord of lords and King of kings—will set His throne atop Zion once He returns. Ezekiel tells us He will rule over the nations from a temple high atop a mountain.

During the Tribulation, God's judgments will dramatically change the topography of the earth. We see this in passages such as Isaiah 24:19–20, Psalm 46:2, and Revelation 6:12–14. Along with restoring the planet after His return, the Lord will raise the Temple Mount so it stands high above the surrounding land.

Isaiah 2:2–3 provides another witness to the elevated place of Jesus' seat of power:

> And it shall come to pass in the last days, that the mountain of the Lord's house shall be established in the top of the mountains, and shall be exalted above the hills; and all nations shall flow unto it. And many people shall go and say, Come ye, and let us go up to the mountain of the Lord, to the house of the God of Jacob; and he will teach us of his ways, and we will walk in his paths: for out of Zion shall go forth the law, and the word of the Lord from Jerusalem.

Early in the Millennium, King Jesus will ascend this high mountain to assume residence in the newly constructed millennial temple. People from all over the world will come to Jerusalem to worship Jesus and learn from Him. For the Jewish people who enter the Millennium in natural bodies, the elevated Jerusalem will signify the magnificent restoration of their kingdom.

After describing the temple and it measurements (Ezekiel 40–42), the Lord spoke directly to the prophet concerning the magnificent location of His throne:

Son of man, this is the place of my throne and the place of the soles of my feet, where I will dwell in the midst of the people of Israel forever. And the house of Israel shall no more defile my holy name, neither they, nor their kings, by their whoring and by the dead bodies of their kings at their high places. (Ezekiel 43:7, ESV)

During this preincarnate appearance, the Lord identified the temple on this high mountain as the place from which He will reign as King over all the peoples of the earth. In the context of Jesus' mountaintop rule, Psalm 48:1–5 comes alive:

Great is the Lord and greatly to be praised in the city of our God!
His holy mountain, beautiful in elevation, is the joy of all the earth, Mount Zion, in the far north, the city of the great King.
Within her citadels God has made himself known as a fortress.
For behold, the kings assembled; they came on together.
As soon as they saw it, they were astounded; they were in panic; they took to flight. (ESV)

This mountain will be so majestic that it will frighten those who are in their natural bodies. What could cause even leaders of the nations to flee at its sight? The presence of God's glory.

THE GLORY RETURNS

By the time Nebuchadnezzar and his armies ransacked and destroyed Jerusalem, God's glory had long since departed from Solomon's Temple, and there's no record of it returning since then. In Ezekiel 10, the prophet describes the exit of God's glory from the ancient place of worship. It's only fitting that the prophet who watched the Lord's radiance depart from Israel should be the one with the vision of it returning to Mount Zion:

> And the glory of the Lord came into the house by the way of the gate whose prospect is toward the east. So the spirit took me up, and brought me into the inner court; and, behold, the glory of the Lord filled the house. (Ezekiel 43:4–5)

Significantly, it was right after God's glory filled this temple that Christ spoke directly to the prophet, declaring that it "is the place of my throne." It's His glory that will shine forth from it to all who gaze upon the mountain.

SIMILARITIES TO THE NEW JERUSALEM

The similarities between Ezekiel's vision of the millennial temple and the New Jerusalem that John describes as recorded in Revelation 21–22 are impressive:

1. In Ezekiel 40:3—14, someone with the appearance of a man measures the dimensions of the future temple. In Revelation 21:15–17, the angel showing the Apostle John the New Jerusalem measures the city.
2. Ezekiel 43:6–12 records the words of the Lord Himself verifying the prophet's vision of the temple and His rule from the mountain. Revelation 22:16 contains the Lord's testimony to the veracity of John's vision of the holy city, as well as to all that he wrote in the book.
3. Just as the Lord's glory fills the temple in Ezekiel's vision (Ezekiel 43:1-4), so God's glory will illuminate the earth from the New Jerusalem (Revelation 21:23–24).

4. A river will flow from both the millennial temple and the New Jerusalem (Ezekiel 47:1–12; Revelation 22:1–2)
5. Jesus will rule over the earth from both places.

THE DIFFERENCE

One key difference disallows any attempt to equate the millennial Temple Mount with the New Jerusalem. Whereas Ezekiel's record provides many details of the structure from which Jesus will reign, John explicitly said our eternal residence will *not* have a temple:

> And I saw no temple in the city, for its temple is the Lord God the Almighty and the Lamb. (Revelation 21:22)

The Apostle John clarified that the New Jerusalem will not contain a temple. Ezekiel's vision is all about the millennial place of worship for Israel. We must not combine the two.

The bottom line is that Jesus' millennial rule from a temple high atop a mountain can't be the New Jerusalem because the Apostle John clearly stated there's no temple in the city. It's impossible to equate the two.

WE WILL SHINE

Another unifying theme between the place of Jesus' millennial reign and the New Jerusalem is that His radiance will brightly illuminate each place. Since we are coheirs of the kingdom along with Jesus, this means we will also shine with God's glory, especially after spending time with our Lord on His Temple Mount.

Did the Apostle Paul hint at this in 2 Corinthians 3:12–18? If Moses needed to put a veil over his face to hide its brightness after being with

God, isn't that same glow what we should expect in our glorified bodies after being with Jesus in His mountaintop home? Then we have these words in Psalm 37:6:

> He will bring forth your righteousness as the light, and your justice as the noonday. (ESV)

The implication of Revelation 19:8 and 14 is that the Lord will adorn us in bright white linen. The Greek word for "bright" in 19:8 is *lampros*, from which we get out word "lamp." The same word is used in Acts 10:30, where the implication is that the angel who appeared to Cornelius glowed in appearance.

Many refer to a "mountaintop experience" today as something wonderful. Christians use the phrase to depict times when they have felt God's presence in a real and unexpected way.

However, nothing in this life can compare to what we will feel when we see the millennial temple high atop a mountain filled with the brightness of God's glory. It's easy to skip over this aspect of our future lives, but it's all a part of the Lord's majestic reign and the awe He will inspire throughout the earth. And, since it will be the place where Jesus is headquartered, we will journey between the mountain and the New Jerusalem on many occasions.

If we were to see Jesus' glory filling the surroundings of His throne with brilliance cascading down the slopes of the mountain with our natural senses, we would panic and run away (Psalm 48:5). But in the future, the spectacle will fill our hearts with wonder and overflowing joy.

Chapter 12

A King with No Equal

The Bible doesn't point you to many heroes. No, there's one
hero in Scripture: the Son, the Lamb, the Savior, the King, the
Redeemer—Jesus.

~Paul David Tripp, Twitter post, March 23, 2023

Revelation 20:1–10 provides a brief overview of what happens
between the Tribulation and the great white throne judgment
that occurs just before the eternal state. Why would John devote such
few verses to describing this glorious time? One reason might be that
so much is written about the Millennium in the Old Testament. The
apostle gave enough detail to determine the place of Jesus' reign in
scheme of prophetic events, and he designated its length as a thousand
years.

As we turn to the pages of the Scripture that were written before
Jesus' birth, we find an abundance of references to His future rule. We
also discover much about His character as King. He will truly be a ruler
like the world has never seen. He has no equal for a number of reasons.

HE IS COMPLETELY RIGHTEOUS

In Isaiah 32:1, the prophet said:

> Behold, a king shall reign in righteousness, and princes shall rule
> in judgment.

The Lord will rule over the nations in perfect righteousness (see also Isaiah 11:4). In contrast to the current heads of countries around the world, Jesus will be a virtuous and moral leader. He will be above reproach in every way, perfect and sinless.

In our current world, when we think about politicians and rulers of this age, the word "liar" frequently comes to mind. We don't trust most of those currently in power over us. However, as God, it will be impossible for Jesus to lie (Titus 1:2). He will always speak the truth; He will be absolutely trustworthy.

Can you imagine a King over all the earth who is incapable of deceiving people?

In our glorified, sinless bodies, we will also be incapable of misleading people. We will be holy and blameless (see Ephesians 1:4). Now, we live with effects of the sin nature we inherited from Adam, but at that time, we will not only share in Jesus' reign, but we will also do so in perfect righteousness.

What an amazing future we have because of the cross where Jesus shed His blood for our sins and we became "the righteousness of God" in Him (2 Corinthians 5:21).

HE IS A BOUNTIFUL PROVIDER

Isaiah 25:6–9 describes a lavish feast the Lord will provide during His reign over the earth. Verse 9 speaks of the joy of being with the One whose appearing we have anticipated for so long:

And it shall be said in that day, Lo, this is our God; we have waited for him, and he will save us: this is the Lord; we have waited for him, we will be glad and rejoice in his salvation.

Some believe the feast described in Isaiah 25 is the marriage supper of the Lamb, which they place early in the Millennium. We, however, see it as an example of the Lord's abundant provision for His people. He will tenderly care for all those alive during this time, whether it be us as the glorified saints of all the ages or the Jews and Gentiles who will enter the Millennium in their natural bodies.

Regardless of where one places the bountiful meal of Isaiah 25:6–9, it speaks of future joy and of a Lord who loves to provide for His own. Could this be one of many such feasts in eternity? Given the nature of King Jesus, it seems quite likely.

In Psalm 36:7–9, David describes the generosity of the Lord toward those who belong to Him:

How precious is your steadfast love, O God!
The children of mankind take refuge in the shadow of your wings.
They feast on the abundance of your house, and you give them drink from the river of your delights.
For with you is the fountain of life; in your light do we see light. (ESV)

Could the above verses also refer to the Millennium? Yes, they describe what life will be like under our kind and benevolent King. The word "abundance" will define Jesus' rule over the nations—both in the Millennium and throughout eternity.

Perfect conditions will exist throughout the earth. Poverty will not be present. Jesus will generously supply the needs of all who worship Him. This, however, will serve as a test for those born during this time.

Will they recognize their prosperity as coming from the Lord, or will they rebel against Him in the end? Stay tuned!

HE IS AN UNERRING JUDGE

In ancient times, difficult judicial cases went to the king of a nation; there wasn't a supreme court. During the Millennium, Jesus will function as the Supreme Judge. Isaiah 11:3–4 provides a clear picture of Jesus as an exalted magistrate:

> And his delight shall be in the fear of the Lord.
> He shall not judge by what his eyes see, or decide disputes by what his ears hear, but with righteousness he shall judge the poor, and decide with equity for the meek of the earth; and he shall strike the earth with the rod of his mouth, and with the breath of his lips he shall kill the wicked. (ESV)

The last lines of verse 4 clearly separate this text from both the Church Age and the eternal state. These things will only happen when Jesus returns to the earth to reign over the nations.

In our day, deception and error can take place in human courts where judges, lawyers, and members of juries are sinful humans who make mistakes at times. This is not so with the Lord. His decisions won't rest on what He sees or hears regarding the case, but on what He knows to be true based on His all-knowing nature as the Sovereign God. Jesus' decisions will be 100 percent correct in every case.

Does that have any significance for us as New Testament saints? Absolutely! In 1 Corinthians 6:1–3, the Apostle Paul described our role as New Testament saints who will reign with Jesus:

Dare any of you, having a matter against another, go to law before the unjust, and not before the saints? Do ye not know that the saints shall judge the world? and if the world shall be judged by you, are ye unworthy to judge the smallest matters? Know ye not that we shall judge angels? how much more things that pertain to this life?

We will settle disputes during our reign with Jesus. Although we will possess unfailing righteousness, the world will be populated by people living in their natural bodies that are capable of sinning, which they will do. Our future part in this regard also includes a ruling aspect, which helps us understand why we will "judge angels" who never sin and thus never need us to intervene in disputes.

Because we will be so much more in tune with the Holy Spirit during this time, we will have the Savior's wisdom in deciding cases brought before us. Just like the Lord, we will never err in our judgments because we will know the truth.

Will we have a role in sentencing the guilty? It's very likely we will. Though not specifically defined in the Bible, it appears that, in our glorified bodies, we will have "supernatural" powers that far exceed the abilities of our natural ones.

HE IS HIGHLY EXALTED

The picture we see in the Psalms about Jesus' rule in the Millennium is one of exaltation and majesty. Psalm 99:1–3 is just a sample of the glory assigned Him:

The Lord reigns; let the peoples tremble!
He sits enthroned upon the cherubim; let the earth quake!

The Lord is great in Zion; he is exalted over all the peoples.
Let them praise your great and awesome name!
Holy is he! (ESV)

Habakkuk 2:14 adds to this lofty perspective of His future rule:

For the earth shall be filled with the knowledge of the glory of
the Lord, as the waters cover the sea.

This has never happened before, but someday it will (see also Isaiah
11:9).

Psalm 47 also speaks about our Lord's elevated status as the future
King "over the nations." It shouldn't be a surprise that so many of the
Psalms look forward to Jesus' millennial rule on the earth since so much
of Scripture refers to the Second Coming and what lies ahead.

(There's an old hymn Jonathan has played hundreds of times on
his trombone; it's titled "Still Sweeter Every Day." As he was writing
this narrative about Jesus and His future exaltation, the words to the
chorus kept coming to mind: "The half cannot be fancied, this side
the golden shore / O there He'll be still sweeter than He ever was
before.)[61]

In Revelation 19:10, an angel said to John, "the testimony of Jesus is
the spirit of prophecy." The study of future things is all about Him and
lifting up His sweet name. During the Millennium, everyone will praise
and worship Him.

Our efforts to remain true to the integrity of Scripture regarding
Jesus' future thousand-year rule over a restored Israel are vital, but we
must not let the details cause us to overlook how all these things magnify
Jesus' wonderful name.

GOD'S PRESENCE ON EARTH

Scripture clearly states that we must only worship God and no one else. The fact that Jesus will require worship during His reign demonstrates His divinity. As He said, "I and the Father are one" (John 10:30). The peoples of the earth will live under the rule of God Himself.

We read of the joy of God's presence on the earth, especially for the nation of Israel, in Zechariah 2:10–12:

> Sing and rejoice, O daughter of Zion: for, lo, I come, and I will dwell in the midst of thee, saith the Lord. And many nations shall be joined to the Lord in that day, and shall be my people: and I will dwell in the midst of thee, and thou shalt know that the Lord of hosts hath sent me unto thee. And the Lord shall inherit Judah his portion in the holy land, and shall choose Jerusalem again.

During the Millennium, Jesus will require the nations, or at least a sizeable number from each one, to come to Jerusalem to celebrate the Feast of Tabernacles, or Feast of Booths (Zechariah 14:16–19). Jesus will withhold rain from the nations that refuse to comply (14:17).

In ancient Israel, this festival looked back to the time when their ancestors had wandered for forty years in the wilderness, living in tents as they traveled from place to place. Why will the Lord insist that all people remember this time during the Millennium? It will compel them to glorify God as the One who has fulfilled all His covenants with His people. The contrast between life in the kingdom and life in the desert will be a reminder of that. For the Gentile nations, the observance will reinforce truths regarding God's power and sovereignty over all the affairs of humankind. Who else could bring slaves out of Egypt and later give them a kingdom displaying His great power and majesty for all the world to see?

The Bible doesn't specify the role we as New Testament saints will have in this celebration or in its observance. However, it seems likely that we might have a part in both of these things, as well as in announcing and organizing the festival.

Although just tidbits of information are scattered throughout Scripture regarding our future roles in Jesus' kingdom, we know the grandeur of this time will exceed our most far-fetched musings. The experiences of this life, even the severest of trials, prepare us for our future place of service during Christ's reign.

PRINCE OF PEACE

The Messiah is described as the "Prince of Peace" in Isaiah 9:6. To establish peace on the earth, Jesus must first judge the kingdom of Antichrist and destroy the armies of the world Satan will gather to Jerusalem in his final attempt to prevent the Lord from ruling over the kingdoms.

At that time, Christ will initiate unprecedented peace that will last for one thousand years. There will be no wars on the earth during that entire period. Psalm 46:8–10 describes the Messiah's inauguration of universal peace:

Come, behold the works of the Lord, how he has brought desolations on the earth.

He makes wars cease to the end of the earth; he breaks the bow and shatters the spear; he burns the chariots with fire.

"Be still, and know that I am God. I will be exalted among the nations, I will be exalted in the earth! (ESV)

Micah 4:3 also refers to this coming time of peace on the earth:

And he shall judge among many people, and rebuke strong nations afar off; and they shall beat their swords into plowshares, and their spears into pruninghooks: nation shall not lift up a sword against nation, neither shall they learn war any more.

Most world leaders say they desire peace, but their actions often lead to war. There has rarely, if ever, been a time when conflict hasn't raged between the nations in the world. The United Nations will never establish global harmony. Antichrist will declare himself to be a man of peace, but he will bring war and death to the world.

The words of Isaiah 54:17 refer to God's protection of Israel after He restores a kingdom to the nation:

No weapon that is formed against thee shall prosper; and every tongue that shall rise against thee in judgment thou shalt condemn. This is the heritage of the servants of the Lord, and their righteousness is of me, saith the Lord.

Of course, God protects both His children and Israel at the current time. This verse, however, refers to Jesus' future rule. It would be foolish for any power to attack Israel when the Lord Himself is its King and Protector. And they will not do so until the end of the Millennium, when Satan is released from captivity.

The Lord will cause all wars to cease at the start of this peace-filled period. The people of Jerusalem and the world will dwell in harmony. Imagine having a thousand years without a war. Ezekiel 37:25–28 describes the future "covenant of peace" God will establish with Israel. Isaiah 54:10 also refers to it with language that exudes His unfailing love for Israel:

"For the mountains may depart and the hills be removed, but my steadfast love shall not depart from you, and my covenant of peace shall not be removed," says the Lord, who has compassion on you.

The words of this passage await a fulfillment! This is the Lord's promise of peace to Israel.

At the very end of the Millennium, a great rebellion will take place, but Jesus will put a quick end to it (Revelation 20:7–10). See chapter 15 for more information on what will happen at the end of Jesus' rule over the nations.

During the entire time of His reign, Christ's holy and just character will be on full display before for all of humanity. The world will see what it's like to have a perfectly righteous King—but will they come to take it for granted?

Chapter 13

WE WILL REIGN WITH JESUS

The church and tribulation saints will co-reign with the Messianic King over the Gentile nations. They will be the King's representative authority and will carry out His decrees to the nations.[62]

~ED HINDSON, *Future Glory*

One of the most exciting aspects of the hereafter is that we will reign alongside Jesus in His earthly kingdom. When we appear before the judgment seat of Christ (see chapter 6), He will assign us roles based on our faithful service. We see this truth brought out in a couple of His parables in which He assigns "authority" based on our stewardship of the gifts He's bestowed on us (Luke 19:11–27; Matthew 25:14-30). In Luke's account, the reward specifically includes ruling over cities.

We find another specific reference to our future kingdom responsibilities in Revelation 5:9–10:

And they sung a new song, saying, Thou art worthy to take the book, and to open the seals thereof: for thou wast slain, and hast redeemed us to God by thy blood out of every kindred, and tongue, and people, and nation; And hast made us unto our God kings and priests: and we shall reign on the earth.

The above words come from the twenty-four elders who represent the Church in Heaven shortly after the Rapture. They see themselves as future "kings and priests" in the Lord's kingdom.

Jesus promises to give the faithful saints in the church at Thyatira "authority over the nations" (Revelation 2:26–27). In those verses, He quotes from Psalm 2:9, which indicates that we will share in Jesus' inheritance of the nations from His Father and will have a role in His kingdom.

Ed Hindson, in *Future Glory*, wrote the following about the future reign of the saints:

> The time of the reign of Christ will include the raptured church that will reign and rule with Him (Revelation 9:14). The resurrected saints of the tribulation period will reign and rule with Christ as well (Revelation 20:4). The living saints who have survived the tribulation, the believers, will go into the millennial kingdom. The generations that they will produce during the thousand years will also be part of the kingdom. While the believers in glorified bodies reign and rule, those in natural bodies live out life on earth, because it is a time of utopia, euphoria, and prosperity, of feast and blessings. There will be no deception. The devil is not there. He is bound in the abyss.[63]

When the Lord assigns us tasks in His kingdom, the fog preventing us from understanding our varied earthly experiences and sorrows will evaporate; we will recognize their purpose to a much greater degree.

Think of Joseph's experiences after his brothers sold him into slavery. He never could have imagined how his service to Potiphar, his management role while in prison, and his faithfulness to God during years of adversity would prepare him to stand before Pharaoh. All of these circumstances played a part in his storybook-like ascension from being in prison to holding a position as second in command over all of Egypt, the most powerful nation on earth at the time. The Lord used Joseph's suffering and leadership skills to equip him for the high place of authority that enabled him to save a great many lives (see Genesis 50:20).

In the same way, Jesus will blend our experiences, gifts, and talents into His Kingdom purposes for us.

OUR HEREAFTER HOME

In chapter 3, we discussed the wonders of the place Jesus is preparing for us in Heaven. We believe this will be our home not only while the Tribulation is taking place on the earth, but also during the Millennium. The "Father's house" Jesus referred to in John 14:2–3 is the New Jerusalem, where we will dwell for eternity (Revelation 21:9–22:5).

What other wondrous city is there in Scripture apart from the New Jerusalem, or what we refer to as Heaven? We find references to it in the book of Hebrews, in particular 11:16:

> But as it is, they desire a better country, that is, a heavenly one. "Therefore God is not ashamed to be called their God, for he has prepared for them a city." (ESV)

The writer of Hebrews again refers to this city in 12:22:

> But you have come to Mount Zion and to the city of the living God, the heavenly Jerusalem, and to innumerable angels in festal gathering. (ESV)

New Jerusalem of Revelation 21 is the "city of the living God" and the same location of the home Jesus is preparing for us. Why would we leave our beautiful home for a thousand years?

We believe God will place New Jerusalem in close proximity to the world during the Millennium. Scripture doesn't say whether it will be visible to those living in natural bodies during that time, but we will see it.

With our glorified bodies, we will travel back and forth between the Holy City, Jesus' temple on the mountaintop, and the earth with ease. Living in Heaven won't interfere with the tasks Jesus assigns us since we will be able to effortlessly go wherever He wants us to serve Him.

We will differ significantly from those dwelling on the earth during the Millennium. To perform our kingdom tasks as coregents with Jesus, we will interact with the people on earth and have a base of operations among them, but earth won't be our home.

Once we've finished our responsibilities on earth, we'll return to our eternal homes, where we will continue interacting with family members, friends, and the acquaintances we form after the Rapture. *We will have much more in common with our neighbors in Heaven than with those on the earth.*

J. Dwight Pentecost wrote that the purpose of the Millennium excludes our inhabiting the earth alongside those who are in their natural bodies:

The millennial age is designed by God to be the final test of fallen humanity under the most ideal circumstances, surrounded by every enablement to obey the rule of the king, from whom the outward sources of temptation have been removed, so that man nay be found and proved to be a failure in even this last testing of fallen humanity. In such a period, when such a program is being executed, it is obvious that resurrected individuals, who need no testing because they are righteous already and who need not be brought into subjection to the authority of the King...can have no rightful place on the earth at that time....

The essential character and purpose in the millennium leads to the conclusion that resurrected individuals, although having a part in the millennium, are not on the earth to be subjects of the King's reign.[64]

As the population of the world grows rapidly, so will the number of our opportunities to exercise authority alongside Jesus. The cities He assigns us to manage might not even exist until decades or centuries after the beginning of His reign.

While we're not performing our kingdom duties or waiting for the opportunity to do so, we will also be free to explore the wonders of the refashioned creation, which the Lord will wondrously restore after the judgments of the Tribulation bring destruction to and upheaval of mountains and islands across the planet. Of course, these "down times" will also allow us to explore New Jerusalem, deepen our relationships with others in the city, and spend time with the Savior atop His mountain.

Our roles of service won't end after Jesus' thousand-year rule, but they will change, because sin, death, and suffering will not be present during the eternal state (Revelation 21:4). During the interlude between the Tribulation and eternity, people in their natural bodies will die and, as we will see, they will rebel against the Lord at the end of this time. During the Millennium, we will reign with Jesus over people capable of resisting our rule. As mentioned earlier, we will judge civil and criminal cases that will arise because of sin's presence.

REIGNING AS SUPERNATURAL BEINGS

As supernatural beings, having become so at the Rapture, we will either be with King Jesus or have continual access to Him during the Millennium. Not only will we be priests, prophets, and kings over all the earth,

137

we will, as children of God, share in Jesus' inheritance. Everything that is His, God our Father gives to us upon becoming His children. We will then come fully into that indescribably magnificent inheritance in the hereafter—the time that begins upon the cessation of the physical life of the believer, or at the moment when Jesus shouts, "Come up here!"

God's great plan was to have a family who would love Him unconditionally, just as He loves us. We are and will be that family, to the joy of our Heavenly Father, throughout eternity.

Imagine… No. We can't even begin to fathom with our finite minds what it means to be in the same standing as the Father's Only Begotten Son in terms of eternity, or even for one second. We accept it by simple faith in the Father's promises, and that's what makes us accepted in the holy, eternal family of the Heavenly Father.

That's what it means to be as one with the Heavenly Father and His Beloved Son. Jesus' words in the moments before He died on the cross for the sins of the world confirm our status as coequals in God's family:

> That they all may be one; as thou, Father, art in me, and I in thee, that they also may be one in us: that the world may believe that thou hast sent me. And the glory which thou gavest me I have given them; that they may be one, even as we are one: I in them, and thou in me, that they may be made perfect in one; and that the world may know that thou hast sent me, and hast loved them, as thou hast loved me. Father, I will that they also, whom thou hast given me, be with me where I am; that they may behold my glory, which thou hast given me: for thou lovedst me before the foundation of the world. O righteous Father, the world hath not known thee: but I have known thee, and these have known that thou hast sent me. And I have declared unto them thy name, and will declare it: that the love wherewith thou hast loved me may be in them, and I in them. (John 17:21–26)

We will enjoy oneness with the Savior forever. While we are in this human flesh, however, our commission, of course, is to share the Gospel with the world, as Jesus taught in Matthew 28:19–20:

> Go ye therefore, and teach all nations, baptizing them in the name of the Father, and of the Son, and of the Holy Ghost: Teaching them to observe all things whatsoever I have commanded you: and, lo, I am with you always, even unto the end of the world.

So, at the moment, we obey Jesus by bringing others to Him as well as by teaching them about the things of the Lord—leading them to maturity in Christ as His disciples.

But during the millennial kingdom, our commission will be beyond anything we can grasp at present with our finite thinking. In the hereafter, there will be no competitors, envy, or jealousy in any of our activity. We will possess the mind of Christ—our thinking will be like that of our Lord and Savior. We will focus on doing His will. Our goals and desires will be precisely the same as His. Our love will be not for ourselves, but for our brothers and sisters—and especially for our Big Brother, Jesus—the King of Kings.

The Millennium and our reign with Christ should excite us and flood our hearts with joy. It's when we will fully realize God's purposes for our experiences in this life, both good and bad.

The words of Ed Hindson explain why we should not only know about our future rule with Jesus, but should eagerly long for it:

> Many people have neglected the study of the millennial kingdom, dismissing it as confusing or unimportant in comparison with the future new heaven and new earth. However, the millennial kingdom offers yet another Bible prophecy that serves a part of the amazing future we will enjoy with Christ....

Further, we should *long* for this time, knowing we will live and even reign with the Lord in a world far better than the one we live in today. We need not fear this future time. Rather, we should anticipate the millennial kingdom with great joy, knowing our Lord will use it to fulfill His promises to rule the earth.[65]

Chapter 14

KINGDOM LIFE

Imagine a world dominated by righteousness and goodness, a
world where there is no injustice, where no court renders an
unjust verdict, and where everyone is treated fairly…. Imagine a
world ruled by a perfect, glorious Ruler, who instantly and firmly
deals with sin.[66]

~ED HINDSON, *Future Glory*

Now that we've examined our responsibilities as coregents with
Jesus during the Millennium, we'll take a closer look at what
Scripture says about life in His kingdom.

The Israelites who survive the Tribulation will inherit a restored
nation (we explained the biblical basis for this in chapter 10). They will
possess the land God originally promised Abraham (Genesis 15) and, as
their population grows, they will fill all the land that's theirs, something
that has never happened, not even during the time of kings David and
Solomon.

The resurrection of Old Testament saints will take place after the
Tribulation (see Daniel 12:1–3). All those who died in faith before the
Day of Pentecost will rise again to everlasting life at that time. The Bible
doesn't specify what they will do during the Millennium, but we can be

sure they will have a vital interest in Israel's restoration and will take part in governing those who inherit it in their natural bodies, having survived Antichrist's deadly agenda.

The majority of those who come to saving faith in Jesus during the Tribulation will be martyred during this time. In the book of Revelation, we read that John refers to a multitude of people in Heaven who have come out of the Tribulation (6:9–11, 7:9–17). Sometime after He returns to earth, Jesus will raise this group from the dead, and they, like us, will also reign with Jesus in His kingdom (Revelation 20:4). They will have immortal bodies like ours.

There will also be a group of people who come to saving faith during the reign of Antichrist who refuse the mark of the Beast (Revelation 13:16–18) and *somehow* manage to survive the worst persecution and direst conditions ever experienced on the earth. This latter group will enter the Millennium in their natural bodies. They will reproduce and fill the earth during Jesus' reign. This is the group over which we will rule alongside Jesus.

SATAN BOUND

One prominent feature of the Millennium is that Satan will be bound, or restrained, the entire time:

> Then I saw an angel coming down from heaven, holding in his hand the key to the bottomless pit and a great chain. And he seized the dragon, that ancient serpent, who is the devil and Satan, and bound him for a thousand years, and threw him into the pit, and shut it and sealed it over him, so that he might not deceive the nations any longer, until the thousand years were ended. After that he must be released for a little while. (Revelation 20:1–3, ESV)

Author Ron Rhodes wrote about our adversary's captivity:

The devil—along with all demonic spirits—will be bound here for 1000 years during Christ's millennial kingdom. This quarantine will effectively remove a powerful destructive and deceptive force in all areas of human life and thought during Christ's kingdom.[67]

Because it refers to Satan's imprisonment, we know Revelation 20:1–10 can't refer to the current Church Age. That's because, in 1 Peter 5:8, we read that, currently, our "adversary the devil, as a roaring lion, walketh about, seeking whom he may devour." That's clearly part of the current battle with demonic forces Paul wrote about in Ephesians 6:12:

For we wrestle not against flesh and blood, but against principalities, against powers, against the rulers of the darkness of this world, against spiritual wickedness in high places.

Despite the devil's absence from the earth, we will face sin and disobedience as we perform our responsibilities such as judging court cases. At the end of one thousand years, the Lord will set him free to test the inhabitants of the earth. Will he be able to deceive people who will have lived their entire lives under the perfect conditions of Jesus' rule? We'll answer that in the next chapter.

RESTORATION OF CREATION

During the Tribulation, wars, along with God's judgments, will devastate the earth's environment. By the time of Jesus' return, the planet will be in desperate need of restoration to make it even habitable again.

143

The Lord will do more than that as He renews creation to its original, pristine state; this is something that only Adam and Eve have ever seen.

Jesus spoke these words to His disciples promising them a role in His millennial kingdom:

> And Jesus said unto them, Verily I say unto you, That ye which have followed me, in the regeneration when the Son of man shall sit in the throne of his glory, ye also shall sit upon twelve thrones, judging the twelve tribes of Israel. (Matthew 19:28)

Notice Jesus used the word "regeneration" to describe the time when they would rule over the "twelve tribes of Israel" in the future. The word in Greek, *paliggensia*, denotes the restoration of nature to its original state. Isn't this the day the Apostle Paul wrote about in Romans 8:19–23?

> For I consider that the sufferings of this present time are not worth comparing with the glory that is to be revealed to us. For the creation waits with eager longing for the revealing of the sons of God. For the creation was subjected to futility, not willingly, but because of him who subjected it, in hope that the creation itself will be set free from its bondage to corruption and obtain the freedom of the glory of the children of God. For we know that the whole creation has been groaning together in the pains of childbirth until now. And not only the creation, but we ourselves, who have the firstfruits of the Spirit, groan inwardly as we wait eagerly for adoption as sons, the redemption of our bodies. (ESV)

For the time being, creation groans under the curse caused by the original sin of Adam and Eve. At Jesus' return, however, He will remove that curse.

Some see a double fulfillment of the Lord's promise to "create new heavens and a new earth" (Isaiah 65:17). This does happen at the start of the eternal state, as recorded in Revelation 21:1, but will it also occur at the beginning of the Millennium? We believe it will; nature will experience a great renewal when Jesus launches His thousand-year reign.

LONGEVITY

A key indication of the Lord's restoration of creation to its original state is the longevity people will experience during the Millennium; it will be similar to the lifespans of the generations before the Noahic Flood.

We read about the extended length of life during the Millennium in Isaiah 65:20–22:

> No more shall there be in it an infant who lives but a few days, or an old man who does not fill out his days, for the young man shall die a hundred years old, and the sinner a hundred years old shall be accursed.
>
> They shall build houses and inhabit them; they shall plant vineyards and eat their fruit.
>
> They shall not build and another inhabit; they shall not plant and another eat; for like the days of a tree shall the days of my people be, and my chosen shall long enjoy the work of their hands. (ESV)

The prophet's words can't refer to the eternal state, because death will no longer exist during that time (Revelation 21:4). Neither can this passage refer to the current age, since people who live to be one hundred years of age today are considered very old rather than young. So, logically, these verses must refer to the time between the Tribulation and eternity.

Those who enter Jesus' earthly kingdom in natural bodies will build homes, work, and raise families. With the perfect conditions of the Millennium, similar to those after Creation, some might live the entire the time. The phrase, "and the sinner a hundred years old shall be accursed," suggests that sin may be a factor with those who die in their youth, such as at age one hundred. The Lord may shorten the lives of those who continually disobey Him.

It will be a far different world than anything we have ever seen, and one that we will enjoy along with those who inhabit the earth. Many of the people we will interact with on the earth will live for many centuries. We will get to know them well!

LIONS, TIGERS, AND ELEPHANTS

We also see the Lord's restoration of nature in Isaiah 11:6–9, which describes profound changes in the way animals will relate to one another as well as to humans:

> The wolf shall dwell with the lamb, and the leopard shall lie down with the young goat, and the calf and the lion and the fattened calf together; and a little child shall lead them.
> The cow and the bear shall graze; their young shall lie down together; and the lion shall eat straw like the ox.
> The nursing child shall play over the hole of the cobra, and the weaned child shall put his hand on the adder's den.
> They shall not hurt or destroy in all my holy mountain; for the earth shall be full of the knowledge of the Lord as the waters cover the sea. (ESV)

Imagine being near a lion that's as tame as a household cat, or petting something as large as a giraffe or elephant. Animals will no longer be afraid of humans, and we will have no reason to fear them—even those

146

that are considered fierce now. Will they have a better understanding of our words? We might have a better grasp of their needs.

This will be the way God intended for the animal kingdom to operate before sin entered the picture and all of Creation felt the impact of the resulting curse. Those entering the Millennium in their natural bodies will be surprised by the changes. But, after a thousand years, will people take these far-fetched realities for granted? We may never have the opportunity to go on an African safari. However, during the Millennium, we will be able to walk among lions, tigers, and elephants. That's something to look forward to!

FULLNESS OF THE HOLY SPIRIT

The work of the Holy Spirit will be more evident during the Millennium than at any other time on the earth. Not only will we experience His fullness as never before, but so will those who enter the kingdom in their natural bodies.

The prophet Joel wrote about the future outpouring of the Holy Spirit upon the people of Israel:

> And it shall come to pass afterward, that I will pour out my spirit upon all flesh; and your sons and your daughters shall prophesy, your old men shall dream dreams, your young men shall see visions: And also upon the servants and upon the handmaids in those days will I pour out my spirit. (Joel 2:28–29)

The context makes it clear that this happens during the "day of the Lord" (v. 31). Peter correctly connected the events on the Day of Pentecost to the work of the Holy Spirit as described in Acts 2:16–21, but the complete fulfillment of this Joel prophecy awaits a future day.

We know this because, in the book of Joel, we read that the Day of the Lord includes God's judgment of the world (2:1–2), the Second Coming (2:30–32), and the restoration of Judah and Jerusalem (3:1–2). Since these events have not happened, we don't yet live in the Day of the Lord. However, we enjoy a foretaste of the outpouring of the Spirit that will happen at that time.

We see this same theme in Ezekiel 36:22–38, which speaks of a future time since Israel has yet to fully experience any of the promises the Lord made in these verses. We share in many of the blessings of the New Covenant promised to Israel such as the indwelling of the Holy Spirit, but its complete fulfillment yet awaits.

The prophet Jeremiah recorded the Lord's prophecy about His presence among the Israelites during the Millennium:

> But this shall be the covenant that I will make with the house of Israel; After those days, saith the Lord, I will put my law in their inward parts, and write it in their hearts; and will be their God, and they shall be my people. And they shall teach no more every man his neighbor, and every man his brother, saying, Know the Lord: for they shall all know me, from the least of them unto the greatest of them, saith the Lord: for I will forgive their iniquity, and I will remember their sin no more. (31:33–24)

The Lord will anoint those in the kingdom He restores to Israel with a special filling of the Holy Spirit. All those living in the land will know the Lord to such an extent that they will not need others to teach them about Him.

Inhabitants of other nations who come to faith in Jesus during the Millennium will have a similar experience as the result of God's Spirit dwelling within them. George N. H. Peters, in his three-volume work, *The Theocratic Kingdom*, defended the dispensational premillennial view when it was first published in 1884. In it, he wrote about the *"remarkable, astounding outpouring of the Holy Spirit* as presented in the Millennial descriptions" (italics in original).[68] The Gentiles will also "rejoice in the light bestowed; and so extended in its operation that the whole earth shall ultimately be covered with glory."[69]

This supernatural fullness of the Spirit will have an impact on us, even as glorified saints. In Romans 8:23, Paul refers to us as having "the first-fruits of the Holy Spirit." The difference in our lives between now and in eternity is that we will no longer labor under the limitations of our current conditions or the remaining presence of sin. During the Millennium, we will experience the fullness of the Spirit in ways that aren't possible now. He will be a constant source of encouragement, needed information and insight, and guidance. We will always have perfect awareness of the Lord's will as we fulfill our responsibilities in the kingdom.

Will we need smartphones during the Millennium? It's very doubtful. Through the Holy Spirit, we will have continual communication with the Lord. He'll keep us informed of everything we need to know.

JOY

All of these factors point to the much brighter day coming, one full of joy and satisfaction. This experience will begin with the Rapture of the Church and continue into eternity. We face many hardships in this life, but someday soon the Lord will replace those trials with never-ending, abundant delight.

In fact, a key theme in the hereafter is joy. Consider David's words in Psalm 16:11:

Thou wilt shew me the path of life: in thy presence is fulness of joy; at thy right hand there are pleasures for evermore.

"Fullness of joy" and "pleasures for evermore" go against our natural tendencies regarding how we view God and eternity. In eternity, we will have immortal bodies capable of enjoying food, wine, and fellowship. Heaven will be an ecstatic experience for us, one full of many enjoyable activities and pleasures—all free from even a hint of sin. It will be impossible to overindulge in Heaven's delights.

> Therefore the redeemed of the Lord shall return, and come with singing unto Zion; and everlasting joy shall be upon their head: they shall obtain gladness and joy; and sorrow and mourning shall flee away. (Isaiah 51:11)

Our bent toward overemphasizing the "spiritual" aspects of eternity comes from the profound influence of pagan philosopher Plato on the early Church, who believed all matter was evil and only invisible realities were good. This caused many theologians of the time to ditch the whole idea of the Millennium because it sounded too "carnal." As a result, they spiritualized biblical prophecy to force it to align with the teachings of Plato.

Augustine, a fifth-century-AD theologian, objected to the whole idea of the Millennium because the thoughts of "carnal banquets" he visualized might be a part of such a kingdom.[70] He said it "would not be objectionable" if somehow "the nature of the millennial kingdom was a 'spiritual one' rather than a physical one."[71] Can you see how the teachings of Plato caused him to reject what the Bible says about Jesus' future reign over the nations?

The problem with Augustine's way of thinking is that the Bible says there will be feasting in Heaven, and if Jesus is preparing delicious meals for us, how can anyone regard that as "carnal"? For those of us who know Jesus as Savior, a time of rejoicing and celebration awaits—and yes, we will enjoy great-tasting food and wine.

In eternity, the flesh that now pushes us to excess will be forever gone. There will be no such thing as carnal pleasure for us because that part of us will no longer exist. Heaven will include many enjoyments for all our senses, all without even the slightest hint of sin. We will see more beauty than ever before and enjoy music as never before. The meals the Lord prepares for us will taste and smell better than anything we've eaten on the earth.

We must always keep in mind that, after the Rapture, we will continually be "holy and blameless" (Ephesians 1:4). We will enjoy the many pleasures of Paradise minus the consequences of having a fleshly nature. Because it's such an important theme, we can't emphasize it enough. We will rule alongside our Savior in perfect righteousness. *We will never sin again.*

Chapter 15

WHY MUST JESUS REIGN FOR A THOUSAND YEARS?

By the establishment of the theocracy on earth for a
thousand years, under the Messianic theocratic King, God
has accomplished His purpose of demonstrating His rule in
the sphere in which that authority was first challenged....
That authority, which Satan first challenged, Christ has now
demonstrated belongs solely to God. God's right to rule is
eternally vindicated.[72]

~J. DWIGHT PENTECOST, *Things to Come*

W hat makes it biblically necessary for Jesus' rule over the nations
to be a thousand years? Why can't the world go directly from
the Tribulation into the eternal state at Jesus' return to the earth?

Most pastors today fall into the amillennial category; they don't
believe in a literal Tribulation or the thousand-year interlude *before* the
eternal state. They errantly claim that God has rejected Israel and applied
His Kingdom promises to the Church, albeit in a spiritual sense. The
wayward teaching that the Church is now God's kingdom is a popular
viewpoint today.

Why explain the biblical necessity of Jesus reigning over a restored Israel in a book that explains our astonishing existence in the hereafter? Along with describing the surpassing delights of eternity, we want believers to have a solid understanding of all the reasons for our blissful expectations. Those who equate the Church with God's kingdom on earth not only negate what the Bible says about the Rapture, but also push our hope of Jesus' return to the far-distant end of the age, thus erasing our thrilling anticipation of Jesus' imminent return.

The ramifications of rejecting belief in a literal, thousand-year reign of Jesus go far beyond theological debates; such teaching shapes the everyday expectancy of the saints and keeps their attention affixed to the things of this life rather than the blessings of the hereafter.

Below are several reasons there must be a time when Jesus reigns over the nations of the world from the throne of David in Jerusalem.

THE WORDS OF SCRIPTURE DEMAND IT

The first reason for believing Jesus will reign for a thousand years is that the Bible says He will do exactly that (see Revelation 20:1–10). God could've orchestrated the future so that the eternal state would start right after the Tribulation, but He didn't. His prophetic program includes Jesus' reign between the Tribulation and eternity.

Further, the Apostle John repeated the length of Jesus' future rule six times, making it clear that He meant for us to know His reign over the nations would last one thousand years.

It's also impossible to combine the biblical descriptions of the Millennium with the Church Age or the eternal state apart from spiritualizing away the clear meaning of the many prophetic texts that refer to Jesus' reign.

Because sin and death will be possible during Jesus' thousand-year rule (Psalm 2:7–11; Revelation 20:7–10), it can't be the eternal state;

such things will no longer be present during that time (Relation 21:4). There must be people alive in their natural bodies during Jesus' millennial reign who not only are able to disobey the Lord, but who also die—despite the fact that many will live for a very long time (Isaiah 65:20–22)

The Bible also tells us that Satan will be bound during the Lord's thousand-year reign, which makes its identification with the Church Age impossible. The Apostle Peter wrote this about our era:

Our adversary the devil, as a roaring lion, walketh about, seeking whom he may devour (1 Peter 5:8).

The devil is most certainly not bound in our day; he's quite active:

And no wonder, for even Satan disguises himself as an angel of light. (2 Corinthians 11:14)

It's clear that we don't live at a time when our nemesis and his hosts are bound or limited in any way. Ephesian 6:12 also makes it clear that we live during a time of spiritual warfare with evil spiritual forces.

The scriptural descriptions of Jesus' thousand-year rule differ significantly from the current age as well as from the eternal state. It's impossible to place the Millennium in either period without changing the original intent of the biblical writers.

GOD'S COVENANT WITH ISRAEL IS UNCONDITIONAL

There must be a time when God restores a kingdom to Israel because God can't negate His unconditional covenants with Jacob's descendants and King David. The gift of the land to the patriarchs and their descendants came with no strings attached. God deeded it to them without any conditions on their behavior. Israel's *enjoyment* of the land was conditional (depending on their obedience to the Lord) but their eternal claim to it was assured under any circumstances.

Scripture refers to the covenant regarding the land as "everlasting" (Psalm 105:7–11), and not only that, but Israel also has yet to possess all that God promised His people in Genesis 15:17–21.

> Never in Jewish history have the Jews possess all of the Promised Land…. For God to fulfill His promise to Abraham (as well as to Isaac and Jacob), there must be a future kingdom.[73]

Psalm 89:20–37 reveals the eternal nature of the covenant God made with King David regarding the establishing of his descendants on the throne of Israel. The words of this passage allow for God dealing with future kings in His dynasty who would turn away from Him (89:30–32). However, Psalm 89:34–37 affirms the eternal nature of His promises to David:

> My covenant will I not break, nor alter the thing that is gone out of my lips. Once have I sworn by my holiness that I will not lie unto David. His seed shall endure for ever, and his throne as the sun before me. It shall be established for ever as the moon, and as a faithful witness in heaven. Selah.

For God to keep His unconditional covenants with both the patriarchs and King David, there must be a Millennium. Those who claim Jesus fulfilled all the covenants with and promises to Israel at His First Advent ignore the words of the prophetic texts that make such an interpretation impossible.

Prolific author and speaker Dr. David Reagan sums up this reason as God's "promises to the Jews." He states further:

The first reason there must be a Millennium is that God has made promises to the Jews which He will fulfill during this time.[74]

GOD'S HOLINESS DEMANDS IT

God's holiness makes Him wholly different from any other being. He's absolute; all created beings derive their existence from Him. What does that have to do with a future kingdom for the nation of Israel?

The Lord Himself gave us the answer:

Therefore say to the house of Israel, Thus says the Lord God: It is not for your sake, O house of Israel, that I am about to act, but for the sake of my holy name, which you have profaned among the nations to which you came. And I will vindicate the holiness of my great name, which has been profaned among the nations, and which you have profaned among them. And the nations will know that I am the LORD, declares the Lord God, when through you I vindicate my holiness before their eyes. (Ezekiel 36:22–23, ESV)

In short, God's holiness *demands* that He restore a glorious kingdom to Israel. It will be His demonstration of all that He is before the nations of the world.

How do we know this hasn't already happened? Because of the list of His promises in Ezekiel 36:22–38. That list includes many things that have never happened in Israel's history:

- He will gather them from the nations and bring them to their "own land" (v. 24).

- He will cleanse them from their sins and give them a new heart (vv. 25–26).
- He will put His Spirit within them (v. 27).
- They will never again experience a famine (vv. 29–30).
- The surrounding nations will recognize the supernatural aspect of Israel's restoration and glorify the Lord as a result (vv. 36, 38).

One item that certainly places these blessings in the future is God's promise to put His Spirit within His people.

> We know from John 16:7–11 that the Holy Spirit could only come in such a personal way after the death, resurrection, and ascension of Jesus. God could not have fulfilled Ezekiel's prophecy before the time of Christ or even while He was walking on the earth, because it points to a time when the Lord will put His Spirit in the hearts of the Jewish people. This could only happen after Jesus' ascension into heaven; the fulfillment of these verses awaits a future time.[75]

The fulfillment of the promises in Ezekiel 36:22–32 couldn't have happened until after Jesus rose from the dead—and we know that hasn't taken place since then. They must await the future restoration of Israel.

The Lord will defend His honor before the nations by blessing Israel during a still-future time of restoration and great blessing (Ezekiel 36:33–38). That such a purpose seems foreign to our way of thinking doesn't change what the Lord says.

When Moses appealed to the Lord's reputation, His holiness, in pleading with Him not to destroy the Israelites after they worshiped the golden calf (Exodus 32:11–14), the patriarch correctly recognized that God's integrity was at stake if He didn't fulfill His eternal promises to Israel. *Because Israel's future restoration will validate His holy character before all the peoples of the earth, it must happen.*

THE PROMISES TO NEW TESTAMENT SAINTS

The Millennium must happen in order for the Lord to keep all His promises to New Testament saints.

"The Millennium is no optional part of God's plan for the end times," states author and prophecy expert Mark Hitchcock. "It must occur for God to keep His promises."[76] The only way to get around this is to apply allegory, or symbolic meanings, to the original intent of the authors of Scripture. However, spiritualizing the text dilutes our hopefulness for what's ahead after this life.

David Reagan wrote the following concerning the certainty of Israel's restoration during the Millennium:

Literal or plain sense interpretation became a cornerstone of the Dispensational Movement that arose in England in the early 19th Century. Its advocates made a clear distinction between Israel and the Church. They rejected the idea that the Church had replaced Israel and that all the unfulfilled prophecies about Israel would be fulfilled symbolically or spiritually in the Church. Instead, they maintained that all the prophecies concerning the end time regathering of the Jewish people and the re-establishment of Israel would be literally fulfilled.

The first best-selling prophecy book in history was *Jesus Is Coming* by William E. Blackstone. It was published in 1878. In his chapter titled, "Israel to be Restored," Blackstone wrote, "Surely nothing is more plainly stated in the Scriptures." The best-selling Study Bible of all times is the one that was produced by C. I. Scofield in 1909, titled, *The Scofield Reference Bible*. In his notes on Ezekiel 37, he stated that the vision of the valley of the dry bones in verses 1-14 was a prophecy about the regathering of the Jewish people to their homeland in the end times. And he asserted that chapters 38 and 39 were about an end time invasion of Israel by a Russian coalition.

The Christian leaders of the mainline denominations laughed at these literal interpretations and boldly asserted that Israel would never exist again. Once the state of Israel became a reality in 1948, these same Christian leaders began to argue that it was just an "accident of history" and not a fulfillment of prophecy!

This is spiritual blindness, and it is very sad since it has resulted in the average Christian knowing nothing about the significance of the re-establishment of Israel as a miraculous fulfillment of Bible prophecy and a sure sign of the Lord's soon return.[77]

Dr. Reagan is absolutely right; those who deny the prophetic significance of Israel's miraculous rebirth as a nation are spiritually blind, and are unable to recognize the voluminous number of signs pointing to the soon arrival of the Tribulation and thus to Jesus' appearing for His Church, which happens before it.

The Bible promises that we will reign with Jesus in His physical kingdom.

JESUS MUST RULE OVER A WORLD THAT REJECTED HIM

Eric Sauer, in his wonderful book, *The Triumph of the Crucified*, explains the biblical necessity of Jesus reigning over the nations:

> Is not the Most High under obligation to give His anointed King the opportunity to prove Himself to be the best Lawgiver and judge, Regent and world-ruler, and the One Who understands how to direct world affairs better than all the hitherto existing

great and mighty ones of the earth, and this especially within the framework of the *old* creation, in which indeed they have lived and have rejected Him as King? And is it not right that after Satan for thousands of years has shown all the world how he can lie and deceive and corrupt the peoples, that God now on His side should show how He, in Christ, can bless and save and give peace, and this likewise on the soil of this *old* world?... Here where Satan has triumphed must Jesus be crowned.[78]

Why will the Lord demand that all the nations come to Jerusalem to celebrate the Feast of Tabernacles (or Feast of Booths) during the Millennium (Zechariah 14:16–19)? Will it be His way of reinforcing to the entire world the truth that the people whom the world rejected and despised are His chosen ones? The nation He brought out of Egypt so long ago now inhabits the land He promised Jacob's descendants from antiquity.

Why would the Lord demand that the nations celebrate this Jewish feast if it were devoid of significance and a validation of His holiness?

Isn't it the same for us? During the Millennium, Jesus will exalt His saints over a world that has oppressed and persecuted them during most of the Church Age. Think of the millions of martyrs who might be in positions of authority over the very descendants of those who killed them. Imagine the many martyred saints in Nigeria, for example, being leaders over the offspring of those who put them to death in this life.

Lest one might think this application is fanciful, consider the words of the Lord in Isaiah 60:14 in reference to Israel during Jesus' rule over the earth:

The sons of those who afflicted you shall come bending low to you, and all who despised you shall bow down at your feet; they shall call you the City of the Lord, the Zion of the Holy One of Israel. (ESV)

It's no small matter that, someday, the Israelites will watch as descendants of the people who oppressed and killed them will worship the Lord in their presence. The most disputed city in the world will become the principal place for worshiping the God of Israel, the True and Living One. All will know Jerusalem belongs to the Lord and the Israelites.

Many fail to see the necessity of the Millennium because they don't fully appreciate the biblical significance of the Lord's promise to the prophet Isaiah (Isaiah 60:14) regarding Israel. It's foreign to our modern way of thinking. But the fact that one cannot see its significance doesn't invalidate the words of Scripture.

We see an illustration of this principle in Hebrews 7:1–10 concerning Abraham's offering of a tithe to Melchizedek. Notice the words in verses 9–10:

> One might even say that Levi himself, who receives tithes, paid tithes through Abraham, for he was still in the loins of his ancestor when Melchizedek met him. (ESV)

It was as if Levi paid the tithe himself, even though many centuries would pass before his birth.

Yes, we will continue to reign alongside our Savior in the eternal state, but in the interim, the nations that once spurned Jesus, Israel, and New Testament saints must see our triumph in the kingdom that's coming, even if it's only their descendants who witness it.

We accept as fact so many aspects of salvation because the Bible says they are true. We don't fully understand all the facets of our redemption, but through faith we accept what the Lord says about them. Our comprehension increases as we grow in our walk with the Lord.

However, when it comes to future things, many spiritualize the words of Scripture because they don't fit into human, or modern, understanding. The very same people who accept by faith what the Bible says about the gift of eternal life refuse to believe, and even scoff at, what God's Word says about our jubilant lives in the hereafter.

THE MILLENNIUM WILL HIGHLIGHT HUMANITY'S SINFULNESS

Jesus' thousand-year rule over the nations will demonstrate the inherent sinfulness of humanity. Despite the pristine conditions of the world, the flawless character of the King, and the binding of Satan and his minions, a multitude of people will rebel against the Lord after He sets the devil free and allows him to roam the earth once again (Revelation 20:7–10). They will believe the devil's lie that God's holding back something that could make their lives better or perhaps more fulfilling.

Author Erich Sauer expands on this:

Yet further, the end of this kingdom shows how hopelessly lost man is by nature. For what does mankind do after a thousand years of perfect Divine government? It rebels against the Lord and in armed millions takes the field against the Most High (Gog and Magog, Rev. 20:7–10). So the last testing by God shows the hopeless wickedness of man.

Even from the most ideal economic and political conditions, from the most abundant proofs of the grace of the Most High, indeed from the direct rule of the Lord Himself, the nations will have learned so little, that at the end, seduced by the Devil, they will rush together in the most fearful of human revolts (Rev. 20:8).[79]

The uprising at the end of a thousand years will not only highlight the innate sinfulness of the human nature, but also humankind's inability to contribute anything to their salvation. As Paul explained in Ephesians 2:8–9, even our faith comes as a gift from God:

> For by grace are ye saved through faith; and that not of yourselves: it is the gift of God: Not of works, lest any man should boast.

At the end of the Millennium, we see the Lord's reason for binding Satan rather than tossing him immediately into the Lake of Fire, which He will do at the end. God will use him to test humanity, and in so doing will prove the need for regenerated hearts.

Despite the pristine conditions of this period and the perfect righteousness of everyone in charge, a number of people will rebel against the Lord when given the chance.

> Yet, at the end, when Satan is released, most people in the flesh will rally to him when he calls the nations to rebellion against Jesus (Revelation 20:7–10). The Millennium will prove that what man needs is not a new society but a new heart.[80]

This last battle will be short-lived; as soon as the multitude gathers in the plain near the majestic mountain from which the Lord reigns, fire will consume them. Satan, the instigator of the rebellion, will meet his final doom in the Lake of Fire (Revelation 20:9–10).

The white throne judgment will take place after Jesus puts down the final rebellion of humanity (Revelation 20:11–15). As the unsaved of all ages stand before Lord and He opens the books of their lives, no one will be able to offer a valid excuse for their rejection of God or the saving message of the Gospel. If they were to use living conditions as an excuse, the Lord would counter that with what happened at the end of His rule over the earth. All other attempts at explanations would result in similar replies.

To summarize, because of the reasons put forward in this chapter, we know there must be a thousand-year reign of Jesus between the Church Age and the eternal state, during which time the Lord will restore a glorious kingdom to Israel.

Chapter *16*

THE DAWN OF ETERNITY

Scripture doesn't tell us what the new earth will look like, but we have reason to believe that it will in many respects be familiar. Jerusalem will be there—albeit an all-new Jerusalem. John's description concentrates on the Holy City, which has streets, and walls, and gates. John also mentions a high mountain, water, a stream, and trees. Best of all it is populated with the people of God—real people we will know and with whom we will share eternal fellowship.[81]

~JOHN F. MACARTHUR, *The Glory of Heaven*

Revelation, the last book of Scripture, is the grand culmination of many ancient and wonderful prophecies. The horrendous events found in Revelation chapters 6–18 have their roots in the Day of the Lord judgments found in passages such as Isaiah 13:9–13, 24:3–23, and Joel 2:1–11. The ancient Scriptures contain many references to the Second Coming and Jesus' rule over the nations as described in Revelation 19:11–20:10.

However, John's vision of the New Earth and New Jerusalem, starting in Revelation 21:1, is all new, especially his description of the magnificent city where we will reside for eternity. We can't fully grasp the concept of life in the hereafter apart from understanding what life will be like *after* the Millennium.

The difficulty in placing a fitting emphasis on this matter comes from the fact that this temporal life is all we know. Our days consist of such things as attending school, pursuing careers, working, raising families, or enjoying retirement. In addition, a host of other activities compete for our attention and direct it toward earth-bound realities.

Yet, the heart of the Gospel consists of Jesus' promise of eternal life to all who believe in Him (John 3:16). Paul made it clear that, apart from our future hope of a resurrection to eternal life, our faith is useless (1 Corinthians 15:19). Living forever is our biblical hope; it's why we look forward to Jesus appearing soon to take us home. A Gospel without such an imminent expectation is just a sanctified version of Joel Osteen's book, *Your Best Life Now.*

In his book *Desire*, John Eldredge quotes physicist Blaise Pascal on this very matter:

> Our imagination so powerfully magnifies time, by continual reflections upon it, and so diminishes eternity...for want of reflection...we make a nothing of eternity and an eternity of nothing.[82]

Eldredge then expanded on that sentiment:

> We make a nothing of eternity by enlarging the significance of this life and by diminishing the reality of what the next life is all about.[83]

We fight the tendency to become preoccupied with this life at the expense of ignoring eternity, no exceptions. In so doing, don't we "make nothing of eternity and an eternity of nothing?" Let's look at some truths about eternity that can help us avoid focusing only on what we see in the here and now, and direct our attention to eternal realities.

DEATH DEFEATED FOREVER

The final defeat of death, the "last enemy," will take place after Jesus' rule over the nations:

> Then cometh the end, when he shall have delivered up the kingdom to God, even the Father; when he shall have put down all rule and all authority and power. For he must reign, till he hath put all enemies under his feet. The last enemy that shall be destroyed is death. (1 Corinthians 15:24–26)

John described the future fulfillment of the above verses in Revelation 20:11–15. During the great white throne judgment, death itself will be thrown into the Lake of Fire. When we get to eternity, death ceases to exist. People will die during the Millennium (see Isaiah 65:20), but not during the eternal state; Jesus will forever have vanquished the frail mortality of both humans and animals.

If one verse sums up our experience in the hereafter, it's Revelation 21:4:

> And God shall wipe away all tears from their eyes; and there shall be no more death, neither sorrow, nor crying, neither shall there be any more pain: for the former things are passed away.

We will explore many more aspects of our amazing future in the pages that follow. However, as you contemplate forever, meditate on the above words, knowing that such a day lies in your future as a child of God.

Note the tenderness of the Lord that's demonstrated by His wiping "away all tears." This is what a compassionate parent does for a grieving or hurt child. At the start of the eternal state, Jesus will sympathetically and personally deal with any remaining sadness and weeping so that it no longer remains a part of our experience.

What a contrast to our current lives, wherein the death of loved ones, sorrow, weeping, and pain are commonplace for all of us. It's difficult to imagine an existence wherein pain and heartbreak will not only no longer exist, but will also be forgotten amid the brilliance of eternity.

In his book, *The Glory of Heaven*, John F. MacArthur includes a sermon by J.C. Ryle, a Church of England bishop during the nineteenth century. His words regarding Revelation 21:4 still speak to our hearts today:

> Blessed be God! there shall be no sorrow in heaven. There shall not be one single tear shed within the courts above. There shall be no more disease and weakness and decay; the coffin, and the funeral, and the grave, and the dark-black mourning shall be things unknown. Our faces shall no more be pale and sad; no more shall we go out from the company of those we love and be parted asunder—that word, *farewell* shall never be heard again. There shall be no anxious thought about tomorrow to mar and spoil our enjoyment, no sharp and cutting words to wound our souls; our wants will have come to a perpetual end, and all around us shall be harmony land love.
>
> Oh, Christian brethren, what is our light affliction when compared to such an eternity as this?[84]

Regardless of our age, health, or circumstances, we share the hope of living forever in the hereafter because Jesus took the punishment for our sins upon Himself on the cross. We don't know what a day might bring forth in this life, but we know there's coming a day when Jesus will welcome us home and our delight will know no bounds. It could happen today!

THE NEW EARTH

The Apostle John didn't tell us much about the new earth. He offered just a few words on it, as recorded in Revelation 21:1, before moving on to describe the New Jerusalem.

> And I saw a new heaven and a new earth: for the first heaven and the first earth were passed away; and there was no more sea.

The first thing that captures the attention is the statement that "there was no more sea." In the New Testament, the word John uses for "sea" typically referred to the Mediterranean Sea. In this context, most believe it refers to the absence of not only large seas, but also of oceans.

In today's world, the huge bodies of water separate people and nations, but that will no longer be necessary in a world where sin, pain, and death don't exist. Wars will be a thing of the past.

Does this mean there will be no more lakes and rivers? That seems unlikely. For example, we know there will be a river flowing through the New Jerusalem (Revelation 22:1). Further, lakes are a key part of creation's current beauty, and there's no reason to doubt they will exist on the New Earth.

We must not let changes and uncertainty about the New Earth discourage us. The same God who created our current world, which has stunning beauty even in its fallen condition, will fashion the New Earth. Note how author John Eldredge puts it:

How wondrous this will be! Creation can be so breathtaking *now*. What shall it be like when it is released to its full glory? Reading the journals of Lewis and Clark's journey across the West, I am filled with longing for what they saw. The Great Plains were filled with wildlife; the buffalo dwelled in herds of hundreds of thousands.[85]

The same God who formed the gorgeous vistas in the Rocky Mountains, with its herds of elk, and the scenic views along the Blue Ridge Parkway, will shape the new creation. That should put our concerns to rest regarding the New Earth. How can its beauty not take our breath away?

RADICALLY TRANSFORMED OR BRAND NEW?

In order to make way for the New Heaven and New Earth, a drastic change must occur. Scripture refers to the destruction of the current earth and heavens in both the Old and New Testaments. Isaiah 51:6 is one such reference:

> Lift up your eyes to the heavens, and look upon the earth beneath: for the heavens shall vanish away like smoke, and the earth shall wax old like a garment, and they that dwell therein shall die in like manner: but my salvation shall be for ever, and my righteousness shall not be abolished

In Matthew 24:35 Jesus referred to the coming change when He said:

> Heaven and earth shall pass away, but my words shall not pass away.

The most familiar New Testament reference to the future devastation of the existing order is 2 Peter 3:10:

> But the day of the Lord will come as a thief in the night; in the which the heavens shall pass away with a great noise, and the elements shall melt with fervent heat, the earth also and the works that are therein shall be burned up.

There is some debate among Bible expositors, however, as to the nature of the coming destruction. Some believe the Lord will destroy everything on the surface of the earth with fire, but that the planet will retain its global shape. All the remnants of the old will be gone, even traces far below the surface, but the form of the current earth will remain, albeit without oceans and large seas. The Lord will thus completely transform the earth and the heavens, but the basic structure will remain the same.

Others, however, maintain that God will completely destroy the entire earth and all the heavens above, and will start over with completely new substances for both. Late author and former professor at Dallas Theological Seminary, John Walvoord, favored this view and provided a scientific explanation as quoted in *Future Glory*:

> Scriptures are strong in their statement of the destruction of the old heaven and old earth...In view of the tremendous energy locked into every material atom, the same God who locked in this energy can unlock it, reducing it to nothing...it is possible that the destruction of the physical earth and heaven will be a gigantic atomic explosion in which all goes back to nothing.[86]

Both views assume major changes take place both on the earth and in the heavens. New Jerusalem, which will remain the same throughout the obliteration of the existing order, will come to rest on the New Earth and provide light for all the nations.

For this massive city, fifteen hundred miles by fifteen hundred miles, to become a part of the new world, significant global changes must occur. The city will replace the high mountain from which the Lord will rule during the Millennium.

Revelation 21:23 alludes to the changes in the heavens by stating that the New Jerusalem will have "no need of sun or moon to shine on it, for the glory of God gives it light, and its lamp is the Lamb" (ESV). Just as there was light before God created the sun and the moon (Genesis 1:3–16), so will it exist without them.

It's possible that, with some sort of canopy over all the earth, the Lord's glory in the city of Jerusalem could provide light for the entire world, even in its current global shape. Because we have such a brief biblical description of the earth during the eternal state, there's far more we don't know about it than what we do.

CONCLUDING THOUGHTS

As we contemplate the replacement of the current order with a New Earth and heavens, we shouldn't forget that the same God is creator of both the old and new. The millennial realm will be even more wonderful than what we see in nature today, and the eternal state will be a step beyond that.

The experience of the Apostle Paul, recorded in 2 Corinthians 12:1–5, helps expand our imagination concerning what lies ahead:

How that he was caught up into paradise, and heard unspeakable words, which it is not lawful for a man to utter.

What Paul saw was so dazzling and spectacular that he either couldn't describe it or (more likely) was instructed by the Lord not to. One has to wonder if this peek into eternity fortified Paul for the great suffering and affliction that would come his way because of proclaiming the Gospel. What wonders and glories must the apostle have seen and experienced to write what he did about it in 2 Corinthians 12?

In chapter 1, Terry related his experience of the hereafter when his heart stopped beating. The excitement he felt caused him to not want to return after it happened a third time. Doesn't that cause us to long all the more for the Rapture and the start of our grand, eternal adventure?

Our anticipation of forever should not only fill us with wonder and hope regarding the boundless joy in our future, but it should also change us. Here's what the Day of the Lord should mean for all believers:

> Since all these things are thus to be dissolved, what sort of people ought you to be in lives of holiness and godliness, waiting for and hastening the coming of the day of God, because of which the heavens will be set on fire and dissolved, and the heavenly bodies will melt as they burn! But according to his promise we are waiting for new heavens and a new earth in which righteousness dwells. (2 Peter 3:11–13, ESV)

Knowing that someday the Lord will destroy all that we see in this current world should change our perspective on life. The Apostle Peter said it should lead to "holiness and godliness."

A focus on Jesus' appearing, the beginning of eternity for us, will have a purifying effect on our behavior:

> Beloved, now are we the sons of God, and it doth not yet appear what we shall be: but we know that, when he shall appear, we shall be like him; for we shall see him as he is. And every man that hath this hope in him purifieth himself, even as he is pure. (1 John 3:2–3)

The fantastic details the Bible reveals about our lives in eternity are not just for our intellect. As we allow these things to saturate our understanding, they profoundly impact the way we live. We get up in the morning knowing that, since what we see is temporal, we place more value on the unseen realities of eternity. We live with the hope that a much better day lies just over the horizon.

Chapter 17

NEW JERUSALEM

People have told me they can't get excited about the New Jerusalem because they don't like cities. But this city will be different—it will have all the advantages we associate with earthly cities but none of the disadvantages. The city will be filled with natural wonders magnificent architecture, thriving culture—but it will have no crime, pollution, sirens, traffic fatalities, garbage, or homelessness. It will truly be Heaven on Earth.[87]

~RANDY ALCORN, *Heaven*

Although the Apostle John saw both God's new creation and the New Jerusalem, he wrote the most about the city in which we will live forever. Most of what we know about it comes from Revelation 21–22 where, as an eyewitness, the apostle outlined a detailed description.

Large cities in America have become cesspools of violence, lawlessness, and previously unimaginable wickedness. It's understandable that the thought of living in a huge city might seem repulsive to many at first. Who would want to live in such a place?

Author Randy Alcorn addresses this faulty concept of the New Jerusalem in the quote at the beginning of this chapter as well as in the following:

> If you think you hate cities, you'll quickly change your mind when you see this one. Imagine moving through the city to enjoy the arts, music, and sports without pickpockets, porn shops, drugs, or prostitution. Imagine sitting down to eat and raising glasses to toast the King, who will be glorified in every pleasure we enjoy.[88]

In his 1933 book, *Lost Horizon*, British author James Hilton gave the name "Shangri-La" to a mystical secluded valley far away from the known world. "In the novel, the people who live at Shangri-La are almost immortal, living hundreds of years beyond the normal lifespan and only very slowly aging in appearance."[89] Even though the attributes of this magical realm fall far short of the wonders of the New Jerusalem, it comes much closer to capturing the essence of our future than do the crime-infested cities in America.

Jonathan can only remember one time when someone preached about the eternal city. It happened at a singles' conference at his church more than twenty-five years ago. The messages thrilled his heart. We pray the following description of our future residence will do the same for you.

GOD WITH US

After witnessing the existence of the "new heaven and new earth," the sight of the New Jerusalem descending to earth captured the attention of the aged Apostle John (Revelation 21:1–2). As the "holy city" appeared, John heard a "loud voice saying:"

Behold, the tabernacle of God is with men, and he will dwell with them, and they shall be his people, and God himself shall be with them, and be their God. (Revelation 21:3)

The major aspect of the New Jerusalem is that God will dwell with humanity there the way He intended to back in the Garden of Eden. His future presence with us will be much more significant than it was in the tabernacle and temples of Scripture, even more than the one from which Jesus will reign during the Millennium. God's residence will be there, and His glory will illuminate the entire New Earth.

In our resurrected bodies, we will be able to do what no other people have ever been able to do: see God in all His glory and survive the experience:

And they shall see his face; and his name shall be in their foreheads. (Revelation 22:4)

Moses could only see the back of God, but as a result of even that glimpse, his face was radiant for days after he descended the mountain. What will it be like to see God's face? Will our faces also shine after we see Him?

The following paragraphs from Randy Alcorn's book, *Heaven*, capture some of the wonder of what it will be like to enter God's presence in the New Jerusalem:

To be told we'll see God's face is *shocking* to anyone who understands God's transcendence and inapproachability. In ancient Israel, only the high priest could go into the Holy of Holies, and he but once a year....

Not only will we see his face and live, but we will likely wonder if we ever lived before we saw his face! To see God will be our greatest joy, the joy by which all others will be measured....

In Heaven, the barriers between redeemed human beings and God will forever be gone. To look into God's eyes will be to see what we've always longed to see: the person who made us for his own good pleasure. Seeing God will be like seeing everything for the first time. Why? Because not only will we see God, he will be the lens through which we see everything else—people, ourselves, and the events of this life.[90]

If the works of God's hands are so spectacular, what will it be like to stand in His presence and see who created such beauty? We will never be the same. Seeing Jesus face to face at the time of the Rapture and at some point being in the presence of God the Father will far exceed our most satisfying moments on earth and will forever shape our future in Paradise.

INHABITANTS OF NEW JERUSALEM

The New Testament identifies all who will inhabit this holy city and experience the myriad eternal pleasures and happiness that will come with our new dwelling place.

1. Those of us who trust Jesus as Savior in this current Age of Grace will reside forever within its walls. We will live in the place Jesus promised to prepare for us in His Father's house (John 14:2–3).

In Christ, we are already citizens of the New Jerusalem. As the Apostle Paul said in Philippians 3:20, "Our citizenship is in heaven, and from it we await a Savior, the Lord Jesus Christ" (ESV). At His appearing, Jesus will make us fit to inhabit Heaven by exchanging our mortal bodies with immortal ones like His (Philippians 3:20; 1 Corinthians 15:50–54).

Those who trust the Savior after the Rapture, the Tribulation saints, will also live in New Jerusalem in eternity with us. John pictured them being there between their martyrdom and resurrection (Revelation 7:9–17; 20:4). During the Millennium, they will also reign with Christ with incorruptible bodies.

2. The Old Testament saints will also reside in New Jerusalem. The patriarchs looked forward to a heavenly "city":

> These all died in faith, not having received the promises, but having seen them afar off, and were persuaded of them, and embraced them, and confessed that they were strangers and pilgrims on the earth. For they that say such things declare plainly that they seek a country. And truly, if they had been mindful of that country from whence they came out, they might have had opportunity to have returned. But now they desire a better country, that is, a heavenly: wherefore God is not ashamed to be called their God: **for he hath prepared for them a city.** (Hebrews 11:13–16, emphasis added)

Daniel 12:1–2 places the Old Testament saints' resurrection after the seven-year Tribulation. Scripture doesn't specify their role in the millennial kingdom or how they will interact with the Jews the Lord delivers from Antichrist, but they will be with us in eternity.

3. The Israelites who recognize Jesus as their Messiah at the end of the seven-year Tribulation will inhabit the land promised the patriarchs in their natural bodies. The Bible doesn't say what will happen to them at the end of the Millennium, but we can be sure God will greatly bless His people.

4. Angels will dwell with us in the New Jerusalem. The tone of Hebrews 12:22 suggests that this is their current residence, and there's no reason to believe that will change in eternity. What will it be like to interact with the angels who now watch over our lives? Will they tell of how they delivered us from harm at critical times? For sure, they will have a unique perspective or what we endure here below.

5. God will reside in New Jerusalem with us. In John 14:2–3, we read that Jesus referred to Heaven as His "Father's house." What happens as described in Revelation 21 is the joining of His glorious city with the earth—the absolute fulfillment of God dwelling forever with human-kind on earth. According to 21:5, Jesus will sit on "the throne" inside the Holy City for all eternity.

John's words detailing the city's gates and foundation underscore our inclusion in the city as well as that of the Old Testament saints. Notice what the apostle stated about its entrances:

> And had a wall great and high, and had twelve gates, and at the gates twelve angels, and names written thereon, which are the names of the twelve tribes of the children of Israel. (Revelation 21:12)

In a similar fashion, John added the following about the names on the foundations of the great city:

> And the wall of the city had twelve foundations, and in them the names of the twelve apostles of the Lamb. (Revelation 21:14)

Take a few moments to imagine rubbing shoulders not only with the saints of the Church Age, but also with the Old Testament heroes that you've read about and studied for many years. What might you ask the Israelites about crossing the Red Sea? Can you imagine talking to Joshua about the collapse of the walls of Jericho? Will it be possible to view videos of these miraculous Old Testament events?

At some point in eternity, we will have the opportunity to talk with some of the ancient prophets such as Daniel, who could fill in more details of his time in Babylon and his night in the lions' den. Imagine conversing with Jacob and Joseph; their adventures in faith have brought great encouragement to a great many people.

Hindson wrote about fellowship we will enjoy in the eternal city:

> Imagine what it will be like to live in the community of the redeemed. In our final glorified state there will be no sin, no death, no heartache, no jealousy, no competition. We will all live for the blessing of everyone else and for the glory of God. In the heavenly Jerusalem all the hopes and dreams of earth will finally be realized.[91]

The possibilities seem endless, but we will have all eternity. The Bible doesn't explain how we, as time-bound creatures, will relate to the passing of time in eternity. Could we even understand such an explanation before we experience it in Heaven? Probably not.

THE WARNING

In Revelation 21:8, Jesus Himself provided a dire warning concerning those who will **not** reside in New Jerusalem:

> But the fearful, and unbelieving, and the abominable, and murderers, and whoremongers, and sorcerers, and idolaters, and all liars, shall have their part in the lake which burneth with fire and brimstone: which is the second death.

At first glance, we might think the above list excludes everyone from Heaven, and we would be correct. After listing similar characteristics regarding those who are unable to "inherit the kingdom of God" (1 Corinthians 6:9–10), Paul added enlightening words:

> And such were some of you: but ye are washed, but ye are sanctified, but ye are justified in the name of the Lord Jesus, and by the Spirit of our God. (1 Corinthians 6:11)

As we will continue to see in the chapters that follow, the New Jerusalem will be a place of eternal bliss and blessings beyond imagination. However, it's only a forever home for those who call out to Jesus in faith during this earthly life. Those who reject His gracious offer of forgiveness will not enter the heavenly city, something they will regret—literally—forever.

John 3:16 says:

> For God so loved the world, that he gave his only Son, that whoever believes in him should not perish but have eternal life.

Jesus endured great agony and died on the cross because no other way existed to pay the penalty for the sins of a lost and condemned humanity. Three days later, He rose from the dead, proving that eternal life resides in Him and no one else.

Just as He said in John 14:6, He is "the way, the truth, and the life." No one comes to the Father, by any way other than through Jesus and the blood He shed on the cross for the forgiveness of our sins.

Note the simplicity of the Apostle John's words:

> And this is the testimony, that God gave us eternal life, and this life is in his Son. Whoever has the Son has life; whoever does not have the Son of God does not have life. (1 John 5:11–12).

Jesus equals eternal life in the city.

If you haven't already done so, please trust Jesus for the forgiveness of your sins and the gift of eternity with Him. Invite Him into your life. We know that "everyone who calls on the name of the Lord will be saved" (Romans 10:13). The Lord changes us after we receive the gift of saving faith; good works can never transform us (Ephesians 2:8–10).

Please call upon the Lord while you have the opportunity to do so; time is running out before the Tribulation begins. Yes, people will turn to Jesus after the Rapture, but you have no guarantee that you will survive the chaos and destruction that will ensue immediately after Jesus takes His Church out of the world.

The cost of delaying may mean you never again have the chance to trust Jesus and receive His gift of eternal life.

Chapter 18

UNPARALLELED SPLENDOR

Paradise will be restored in the holy city. The biblical story of the human race begins in the garden and ends in the eternal city. In between stands the cross of Jesus Christ. He alone has changed the destiny of the human race.[92]

~ED HINDSON, *Future Glory*

The Bible doesn't tell us everything God revealed to the patriarchs about eternity. The words of Hebrews 11:13–16, however, suggest that Abraham, Isaac, and Jacob know more about the hereafter than Moses revealed in the book of Genesis. They desired a "heavenly" dwelling, a city that God had "prepared for them" (v. 16). They would die long before their descendants possessed the land, but they had the promise of a "city," which we know as New Jerusalem.

In Genesis 11:1–9, ancient globalists who settled in the plain of Shinar not only were building a tower, they were establishing a city. They gave up that effort, however, after the Lord confused their languages and dispersed them (v. 8). Living close to that time period and possibly close to the site of the Tower of Babel, Abram knew about these things before God called him and later changed his name to Abraham.

187

At some point, the Lord told the patriarch about a heavenly city He was preparing for him, and Abraham believed. Just like Abraham, we walk in faith regarding our hope of residing inside the heavenly city, but we have an advantage over the Old Testament saints. We have John's description of our future home.

Throughout the book of Revelation, John functioned as a scribe, writing down future events he witnessed firsthand; in addition, he faithfully jotted down the words he heard. In the last couple of chapters, he had the challenge of infusing eternity into the limited vocabulary of the late first century AD.

AN ANGEL MEASURES THE CITY

As if to underscore the physical nature of the New Jerusalem, the angel speaking to John used a "golden" rod with which he measured "the city, and the gates thereof, and the wall thereof" (Revelation 21:15). The verses reveal its key dimensions:

> The city lies foursquare, its length the same as its width. And he measured the city with his rod, 12,000 stadia. Its length and width and height are equal. He also measured its wall, 144 cubits by human measurement, which is also an angel's measurement. (Revelation 21:16–17, ESV)

New Jerusalem will be huge. The "12,000 stadia" (or "furlongs" in the King James Version) equate to as much as 1,500 miles as its width, length, and height. It's a gigantic cube. Some commentators estimate the distance in each direction at about 1,380 miles, as there's some variation regarding the precise nature of the "stadia" used in ancient times. With either distance, there's nothing with which we can compare it to today.

If we were to superimpose New Jerusalem on the current continental United States, it would stretch from the Canadian border to the Gulf Coast and take up about half of the country's width. Not only that, but it would also be higher than anything we can imagine on the current earth.

Although some think the city might be in the shape of a pyramid, we regard it as a cube. The late commentator Henry M. Morris explained the reason:

> The pyramid shape…(whether as in Egypt, Mexico, or stepped-towers of practically all ancient nations), seems always to have been associated with paganism, with pyramid's apex being dedicated to the worship of the sun, or of the host of heaven….
>
> The cube…was the shape specified by God for the holy place…in Solomon's temple (1 Kings 6:20), where God was to "dwell" between the cherubim. Both the language and symbology thus favor the cubical, rather than the pyramid shape.[93]

The cube shape will not only be fitting for a city hosting God's eternal presence, but it will also suit our ability to move with ease in any direction, including up and down, as glorified beings with at least some supernatural abilities.

> It should be remembered that the new bodies of the resurrected saints will be like those of angels, no longer limited by gravitational or electromagnetic forces as at present. Thus it will be as easy to travel vertically as horizontally in the new Jerusalem.[94]

The dimensions make it clear that there will be plenty of room for everyone to have a spacious dwelling place in New Jerusalem. The thickness of the walls, at 144 cubits, in US measurements would be the equivalent of seventy-two yards. Imagine fortifications almost as thick as the length a football field!

In Revelation 21:18, John added a further description of the barrier separating the city from the outside world:

> And the building of the wall of it was of jasper: and the city was pure gold, like unto clear glass.

The translucent quality of the jasper walls and streets of pure gold will allow God's glory—the sole light source—to shine throughout the entire city as well. We may not be able to fully picture this scenario, but John's words indicate that the wonders of the eternal state will exceed the most beautiful sight we have seen in our lifetimes.

The apostle's description of New Jerusalem stretches our imagination; it's difficult to conceive of such a city that will light up the entire planet. Pastor and author John MacArthur adds his thoughts in this regard:

> Human language is inadequate to fully describe the unimaginable magnificence of the believers' indescribable eternal home. Unwilling to take the language of Scripture at face value, many seek for some hidden meaning behind John's description. But if the words do not mean what they say, who has the authority to say what they do mean? Abandoning the literal meaning of the text leads only to baseless, groundless, futile speculation. The truth about the heavenly city is more than is described, but not less and not different from what is described. It is a material creation, yet so unique as to be unimaginable to us. The words of John provide all the detail we have been given by God to excite our hope.[95]

THE CAPITAL CITY OF ETERNITY

John described the city's foundation as being adorned with many precious jewels (Revelation 21:19–21). From the outside, the sight of the city will be breathtaking.

The Bible doesn't say anything about the people and nations that will inhabit the earth during the eternal state. We can safely assume they will be the ones who remain faithful to the Lord during Satan's final test of the nations at the end of the Millennium (Revelation 20:7–10). Will these saints go into eternity in natural bodies? Will the population of the earth grow during that time? These are possibilities, but Scripture doesn't give us definitive answers.

We know sin, death, and suffering will no longer exist in eternity. In Revelation 21:24–26, John wrote about the monarchs of the eternal state:

By its light will the nations walk, and the kings of the earth will bring their glory into it, and its gates will never be shut by day— and there will be no night there. They will bring into it the glory and the honor of the nations.

The word "nations" typically refers to Gentiles in Scripture, and that appears to be the case here. Those who live during the Millennium and continue into the hereafter will fully participate in the wonders of New Jerusalem. It will be their capital city even if they don't reside within its walls.

The fact that we will rule with Jesus doesn't preclude the existence of kings on the earth during this time. We also see this in Psalm 48:4–5, a passage that fits with Jesus' millennial rule. Those in natural bodies will select local rulers like themselves, but they will be subject to those of us whom the Lord places in charge of the areas we govern.

Because sin will no longer be present, there will be no reason to close the gates of the eternal city. They will be open to all who want to enter. Even if people continue to exist in their natural bodies, they will no longer pass on the sin nature to their offspring. The Lord will remove all the curses that resulted from the Fall (Genesis 3). It still stretches the imagination to conceive of a time when sin and death are not only vanquished, but are no longer even possible.

As if to underscore this, John said:

Nothing unclean will ever enter it, nor anyone who does what is detestable or false, but only those who are written in the Lamb's book of life. (Revelation 21:27, ESV)

Since the unsaved will have already met their fate at the great white throne judgment, it will no longer be possible for any unholy person to enter the city.

The description of the New Jerusalem in Revelation 22:1-2 is encouraging as well as a bit confusing:

And he shewed me a pure river of water of life, clear as crystal, proceeding out of the throne of God and of the Lamb. In the midst of the street of it, and on either side of the river, was there the tree of life, which bare twelve manner of fruits, and yielded her fruit every month: and the leaves of the tree were for the healing of the nations.

The presence of a river and a tree seems familiar. Some of our most treasured vistas on earth involve rivers surrounded by trees and other vegetation. The beauty of nature will be present inside the New Jerusalem.

John's description, however, raises some questions. Will there just be one large tree or many? Some expositors believe many trees bearing fruit that we will eat will line the sides of the river running through the city. Why the mention of just one tree?

Most prophecy commentators believe the reference to the "tree of life" doesn't mean there will be one solitary tree in all the New Jerusalem, but that the "tree of life" will be the one from the Garden of Eden.

Our future paradise will have many features of the one Adam and Eve enjoyed before they sinned. Ed Hindson described it this way:

> The final chapter of Revelation indicates the eternal city will be returned to the inherent qualities of the Garden of Eden—only on a grander scale. Then, and only then, will the Creator's true intention for humanity finally be realized. There in the center of the New Jerusalem, John the revelator sees the *river of life* flowing from the throne of God and the Lamb (v. 1). It is the source of all life that emanates from God Himself.[96]

When believers think of living in a huge city for eternity, they mistakenly picture a sterile environment similar to what they have seen on the earth. Yes, we will live in places that Jesus has prepared for us. However, that doesn't preclude the existence of a lush park alongside the river that runs through New Jerusalem. Assuming God's throne is in the middle of the city, the river might run for up to 750 miles on each side exhibiting the beauty of nature beyond what we have ever seen. We will never tire of spending time there.

John MacArthur offers the following insight about the mention of "healing" in the opening verses of Revelation 22, which can be puzzling at first since it's referring to the eternal state:

> Then John makes the intriguing observation that **the leaves of the tree were for the healing of the nations.** At first glance, that seems confusing, since obviously there will be no illness or injury in heaven that would require **healing.** *Therapeia* (**healing**),

however, does not imply illness. Perhaps a better way to translate it would be "life-giving," "health-giving," or "therapeutic." The **leaves of the tree** can be likened to supernatural vitamins, since vitamins are taken not to treat illness, but to promote general health. Life in heaven will be fully energized, rich, and exciting.[97] (Boldface in original)

LIFE IN THE ETERNAL STATE

What begins in the Millennium will be a warm-up for what comes later. The closing words of Revelation 22:5 state that we will "reign forever and forever." Not only will we rule alongside the Lord during His interim thousand-year kingdom, but our roles will continue throughout eternity.

Our continuing reign with the Savior points to the likelihood of people on earth transitioning from the Millennium to the eternal state in natural bodies. Although we will no longer deal with people being capable of disobeying the Lord—or our instructions, for that matter— they will continue to need our guidance, oversight, and teachings about the Lord.

Eternity will be thrilling. The amazing beauty of New Jerusalem, the glory of God's unending presence, and the wonder of the New Earth will be ours to enjoy forever...and we will!

During our remaining time in this life, we will experience sorrows, pain-filled days, and challenging times. The glimpses of eternal bliss that we see through the eyes of the Apostle John bring light to our dark days. They remind us that the exciting adventure ahead is one that will forever satisfy our deepest longings; we will never run out of reasons to rejoice and praise our wonderful God and Savior.

The more we learn from the pages of Scripture about the joy set before us, the more adept we become at looking beyond our trials to what awaits us in the hereafter.

Chapter 19

KEEP OUR EYES ON THE PRIZE

I press toward the mark for the prize of the high calling of God in Christ Jesus.

~PHILIPPIANS 3:14

We live in a world where everything shouts for our undivided attention. The temptation to forget about what happens in the hereafter has never been greater as we respond to the latest text or hear details about events just minutes after they occur. Smartphones can be great tools, but they also tend to keep our minds focused on what we can see, news from friends and relatives, and—for some—the latest news from our nation and around the globe.

How do we keep our eyes on the prize, the joy set before us at the appearing of Jesus? Nineteenth-century English preacher Charles Spurgeon offered an excellent answer: "Hold everything earthly with a loose hand; but grasp eternal things with a death-like grip."

In other words, it's not that we shouldn't plan ahead or set goals, but we should hold our temporal aspirations loosely in our hands. We mustn't shirk our responsibilities, but live with the mindset Paul wrote about in Colossians 3:1–4:

If then you have been raised with Christ, seek the things that are above, where Christ is, seated at the right hand of God. Set your minds on things that are above, not on things that are on earth. For you have died, and your life is hidden with Christ in God. When Christ who is your life appears, then you also will appear with him in glory.

The first clue to maintaining a heavenly perspective is to keep in mind the above words: We will someday soon "appear with him in glory."

GLORY BEYOND IMAGINATION

Despite the perilous times in which we live, many believers in America continue to enjoy comfortable lives, especially if they remain in good health. Our affluence makes it difficult to fully understand that a much, much better life awaits us in eternity. That's perhaps the main reason many saints remain uninterested in biblical prophecy and don't like hearing that we're living in the last days.

Another reason for such ambivalence is that we often don't appreciate the weight of the word "glory." It's especially hard for believers who never hear about the biblical truth of the hereafter. They hear the words "eternal life" in church, but, in too many cases, no one tells them about the upcoming joy making it necessary to rely on a book like this or listen to prophecy speakers online in order to understand the full importance of those words.

Even as writers, we struggle to find words that adequately convey the wonders and spectacular nature of Paradise. No one currently living on earth, regardless of their great wealth, has anything close to the amazing lifestyle we will experience for eternity.

Many people regard the Rapture as an unwanted interruption. However, those who understand the spectacular nature of existence that will begin with Jesus' appearing often pray for it to happen soon. The difference between these attitudes lies in grasping what the Bible says about what happens after Jesus catches us up to meet Him in the air (1 Thessalonians 4:17).

BOUNDLESS JOY

We have purposely emphasized the hereafter's aspect of joy in this book. Our time in Heaven while the Tribulation is playing out on earth will be one of jubilant celebration and praise for our Lord. We can't say it enough: Our lives in eternity will be far more delightful than we can fathom with our limited perspective.

Please don't let the negative, false caricatures of Heaven discourage you. We will most certainly not be lonely harp players on clouds. Many saints endure the pangs of loneliness in this life, but they'll never again have to endure that pain in Paradise. We will be surrounded by many other saints and enjoy reunions with family members and friends.

Heaven won't be boring, as some imagine. Its splendor will stun us upon our arrival, and there will always be new wonders to take in, people to talk with, and comforts of home to enjoy.

Randy Alcorn addresses the fallacy that our lives in the hereafter will be monotonous or even boring:

Our belief that Heaven will be boring betrays a heresy—that God is boring. There's no greater nonsense. Our desire for pleasure and the experience of joy come directly from God's hand. He made our taste buds, adrenaline, sex drives, and the nerve endings that convey pleasure to our brains. Likewise, our imaginations and our capacity for joy and exhilaration were made by the very God we accuse of being boring. Are we so arrogant as to imagine that human beings came up with the idea of having fun?[98]

Those who view Heaven as a place of great, unending joy have comfort during trying times here below.

IMMORTAL BODIES

Many saints fail to focus on eternal realities because they don't fully understand the marvelous nature of the new bodies Jesus will give us at the time of the Rapture. These bodies will be immortal and incorruptible. We get a sense of Paul's enthusiasm regarding this expectation in Philippians 3:20–21:

> But our citizenship is in heaven, and from it we await a Savior, the Lord Jesus Christ, who will transform our lowly body to be like his glorious body, by the power that enables him even to subject all things to himself. (ESV)

Shortly after the apostle referred to the "prize" before him, he spoke of Heaven, Jesus' appearing, and his own receipt of a "glorious body." He served the Lord through much affliction knowing that a much better day was just ahead (Romans 8:18). The Rapture was the "prize" that occupied his thoughts as he suffered in the earthly realm for the cause of Christ.

Paul wrote that our future bodies will be like the one Jesus had after His resurrection. Even if you are young, healthy, and strong, the body Jesus will give you at His return will be a vast improvement. Those of us who are older look forward to the complete health we will enjoy along with the absence of all the effects of the aging process. We will regain an appearance of youth, with perfectly whole bodies that will never experience any type of sickness.

Forget about looking for a fountain of youth and enjoy getting older. Jesus will give believers a body like His when He takes us home. What about children at the time of the Rapture? Will they continue to grow, or will they suddenly become young adults in appearance? Although the Bible doesn't address this matter, Jesus' special love and care for children favors the first alternative, with them maturing after they arrive in Paradise.

Our glorified bodies will have abilities that far exceed any we could ever have in this life. As mentioned, we believe we'll be able to swiftly move between earth and New Jerusalem, as well as anywhere inside the huge city, during the Millennium. We will also have remarkable discernment skills that will help settle disputes among the Tribulation saints during those thousand years. Our unique skills may include powers to enforce our decisions, even in criminal cases that come before us.

Our future bodies will have many similarities to our current ones, including being physical rather than spiritual entities, just as Jesus' body was after His resurrection (Philippians 3:20–21). Further, when Jesus appeared to His disciples, He emphasized that He was not a "spirit" and encouraged them to "touch" Him. He also ate in their presence (Luke 24:36–42), and later cooked breakfast on the beach for some of His followers, at which time we can safely assume He ate with them (John 21:11–15).

On a light note, there's something our homes now have that will be missing in the place Jesus prepares for us in Heaven: toilets! We won't need them with our glorified bodies even though we will forever enjoy both food and drink.

Just as with the Lord, our acquaintances, friends, and family members will recognize us in eternity, and we will be able to identify them. We'll remember people long forgotten, because in eternity, the Holy

Spirit will enhance our already rejuvenated minds. Don't worry about forgetting names, like so many of us do! In Heaven, we will recognize everyone.

Any-Moment Transformation

Once we realize that we could instantly find ourselves in the presence of our Savior (Colossians3:4), we pay more attention to our hope on a daily basis.

The Rapture can occur at any moment. As the signs of the coming Tribulation period multiply like bugs attracted to bright lights on dark summer nights, we know His appearing is near. We worked on this book with the realization that the Lord might very well catch us up to meet Him in air before we finished writing or prior to its publication. We know He is coming soon, but we keep serving Him in the meantime.

We most certainly live in the season of Jesus' return to take His Church back to Heaven. Any day could be our last on earth. See appendix B for twelve unmistakable signs pointing to the nearness of the Day of the Lord and hence to the Rapture, which happens before its start.

Perfect Holiness

As New Testament saints, we stand holy and blameless before God. He has completely forgiven *all* our sins and cancelled the debt that came with them (Ephesians 1:4; Colossians 2:13–14). Our redemption is both complete and sure.

In eternity, we will not only be free from the penalty of sin, but we'll also be forever removed from its presence. Can you fathom being righteous and forever incapable of sinning? None of the residents of New Jerusalem will ever transgress or disobey the Lord again.

Think about it: No more locked doors! The residents of the eternal city won't steal anything from us, nor will they harm us in any way. Everyone there will be unable to sin, just like us.

PERFECTED RELATIONSHIPS

Because we will forever be free from the presence of sin, our relationships in Heaven will be all that God intends. Although we won't remain married in Heaven (Matthew 22:30), we will know our spouses and spend time with them just as we will with all of our other loved ones.

Our interactions with everyone will improve, because all the attitudes and sins that currently cause problems will cease to exist. Selfishness, envy, disgust, and seeking revenge will no longer exist in the hereafter.

INHERITING A KINGDOM

Have you ever toured a parade of homes? It's an event that allows homebuilders to display their latest projects. For a fee, the public is allowed to visit these typically fabulous places to live.

Jonathan and his wife participated in a parade of homes several years ago, and enjoyed seeing the beautiful houses even though they couldn't imagine living in them because they knew they could never afford them. Sometime later, in the process of moving from Iowa to Illinois, they purchased a home that was still under construction. Their approach to the new residence was much different than it had been when they had viewed the showcased homes. Knowing they would soon own their new dwelling, they *did* imagine living there. They planned the location of furniture and belongings, and envisioned what it would be like to live there.

The same is true of the kingdom we will inherit. Once we grasp that it will be ours someday, our curiosity grows. We pay attention to what Scripture says about our future legacy. We look for those who can help us better understand what it will mean to reign alongside the Savior.

Doesn't this also explain why, since the early centuries of the Church, Satan has fought to keep believers from reveling in their anticipation of the hereafter? He hates the idea of the Lord ruling over his current domain and never stops trying to distract believers from this wondrous anticipation. He lures many into falsely believing the Church rather than Israel is the fulfillment of God's Old Testament kingdom promises.

What does it matter what we believe about Jesus' reign on the earth? Our inheritance in the coming kingdom not only adds a forward-looking perspective to our daily lives, but provides a powerful added incentive to serve Jesus. It's the difference between looking at a gorgeous home knowing it is far beyond our budget and reading about a glorious kingdom knowing that we are coheirs of it in Christ (Romans 8:17; 1 Corinthians 15:50–54).

We also have the added incentive of hearing Jesus say the words, "Well done, good and faithful servant, thou hast been faithful over a few things, I will make thee ruler over many things: enter thou into the joy of thy lord" (Matthew 25:23) at the judgment seat of Christ. Our faithful service in this life brings both the Lord's approval and assignment of service in the kingdom.

Yes, we seek to please Him because of our love for Him in light of His great sacrifice so that we might have eternal life. However, amid the many challenges we face here below, it's more than a little comforting to know that, in the end, what counts is Jesus' assessment of our service for Him and our inheritance of a kingdom.

We often find it difficult to make sense of many events and circumstances in this life, but when the Lord assigns us a place in the coming kingdom, we will see all the more clearly the reasons for the afflictions He sent our way or allowed to happen. Just like He used all of Joseph's hardships to prepare him to reign alongside Pharaoh, so He's using our suffering and experiences to prepare us for our future inheritance.

What might we do during our reign with Jesus? Based on what the Bible says and what this time might look like, we will:

1. Rule over cities.
2. Judge disputes and reside over criminal cases (1 Corinthians 6:1–3).
3. Enforce the decisions we make pertaining to matters of the law.
4. Instruct the nations in the way of the Lord.
5. Inform people of upcoming events such as the Feast of Booths.
6. Function as the Lord's messengers.

We no doubt will also have many other fulfilling and important tasks as well.

WE WILL BE HOME

Home. The place Jesus is preparing for us will satisfy every longing and need we've ever had…forever. That might seem impossible to many of us now, but the One who's making it ready for us not only knows what we will be like in eternity, but He also understands us better than we do ourselves.

As the path for believers on earth grows increasingly tough to navigate, the anticipation of going to our eternal home grows all the stronger.

Almost thirty years ago, Jonathan spent an afternoon with his friend Al just days before cancer claimed his life. Al's heart was set upon Heaven. He not only longed to see Jesus, whom he loved, but understandably he also wanted his intense pain and suffering to end. During his final days, he repeated these words a great many times: "I want to go home!" Everyone around him recognized the faith behind his request.

After this life is over, Jonathan will again visit with Al—in Heaven. His resurrected body will be vastly superior to the one in which he spent his last agonizing days on earth. His smile will speak volumes as they catch up with each other about the intervening years. He's home now, but an even more glorious day awaits him as the Lord gives him an imperishable body.

The word "home" sums up our glorious hope. Once we arrive there, the suffering, pain, afflictions, illnesses, and sorrows will all be remnants of the past that will never again afflict us.

The presence of lawlessness, deception, and wickedness beyond what we ever could've envisioned even just twenty years ago also causes many of us to yearn for home with each news report that comes our way.

For those of us in Christ, a great prize awaits. It begins with God's upward call at the time of the Rapture and gets even better after that. The hereafter is not some pie-in-the-sky promise; it's reality. We are heirs to a kingdom. Our eternal prize is perhaps just a heartbeat away.

Chapter 20

FREQUENTLY ASKED QUESTIONS ABOUT HEAVEN

One of the most incredible prophecies in the Bible is the coming of the kingdom of Christ on the earth. Those of us who believe in the rapture are often criticized for being escapists who want to abandon the planet God created. In reality, nothing could be further from the truth. We actually believe we are coming back to reign with Christ for one thousand years during His millennial kingdom.[99]

~ED HINDSON, *Future Glory*

Throughout *Hereafter*, we've tried to provide a biblical picture of our glorious hope and what we can expect after the trumpet sounds and the Lord catches us up to meet Him in the air. However, we suspect that many of our readers may still have questions about the hereafter.

For that reason, we've compiled a list of answers to frequently asked questions related to what the Bible teaches about our life in Paradise. We've already answered some of them in preceding chapters, but include them again for easy reference.

Q. Where can we find out about eternity?

A. Scripture is the sole source and authority for what we will experience in the afterlife. Throughout this book, we've strived to base everything on what the Bible says about eternity and what we can safely infer from its words.

We have strived to base our viewpoints regarding the Rapture, Tribulation, Second Coming, Millennium, and eternity upon God's Word. We place a high importance on the words of Scripture and upon which we base our understanding of the hereafter.

The words of Scripture matter; they must be our sole source of what to expect in eternity. The spiritualizing of the prophetic texts allows the interpreter to decide what lies ahead for believers. Proverbs 30:5 says, "Every *word* of God proves true" (ESV, emphasis added).

Q. What is Heaven?

A. At the time of the Rapture, the Lord will catch us up in the air and take us to His Father's house in Heaven (John 14:2–3). During the seven-year Tribulation on earth, we will reside in the place He's preparing for us. Our residence in this city will also be our home during the Millennium and throughout eternity.

In the eternal state, Heaven will be the New Jerusalem, with streets of translucent gold and thick walls of clear jasper, but it will also include the New Earth, which we will have access to forever. Both realms will be a forever Paradise for all the redeemed to enjoy. The glory of this city will far surpass even our most fantastic concepts of it; we won't be disappointed, not in the least.

Q. Will Heaven be boring?

A. Many folks often regard Heaven as a boring place. But nothing could be farther from the truth. Worship will be action, an unstoppable response to the glories of Heaven and the full realization of all the Lord is and does. We will explode with a desire to serve Him in any way He wishes. We will experience magnified heavenly desires once we're at rest in our eternal home.

Randy Alcorn, in his book, *Heaven*, addresses the fallacy that eternity will be monotonous:

> Our belief that Heaven will be boring betrays a heresy—that God is boring. There's no greater nonsense. Our desire for pleasure and the experience of joy come directly from God's hand. He made our taste buds, adrenaline, sex drives, and the nerve endings that convey pleasure to our brains. Likewise, our imaginations and our capacity for joy and exhilaration were made by the very God we accuse of being boring. Are we so arrogant as to imagine that human beings came up with the idea of having fun?[100]

In Psalm 16:11, David confirmed this upbeat view of eternity:

> In your presence there is fullness of joy; at your right hand are pleasures forevermore.

If the Lord wanted our joy to be full through answered prayer in this life (John 16:24), how much more should we expect when we arrive in Heaven—where we'll be free from sin and from all that robs us of happiness here below?

Q. Will Heaven be a long worship service?

A. Some believers have a dim view of Paradise because they view it as one long worship service wherein they will grow weary of standing and singing for long hours at a time.

Several factors refute such sentiment:

First, our adoration for the Lord will not be obligatory, nor will it be confined to a "service." Our worship will be an ongoing, unstoppable response to all we will see and experience in glory. We will understand, as never before, all that Jesus gave up in order to come to earth, suffer, and die on the cross so that we might *possess* that eternal life. Simply being in the presence of God the Father will compel us to continually respond with adoration. We won't be able to hold back the praise that will well up inside of us!

Second, Jesus is preparing a place for us in His "Father's House" (John 14:2–3), suggesting that our time (in whatever sense that is conveyed in eternity) won't be limited to one specific activity; we will enjoy the many facets of our forever home as well the glorious city in which we will live.

Third, our time in Heaven while the Tribulation takes place on earth will be a time of rest from all that happened in our mortal lives and a period of preparation for the roles the Lord has for us when we reign with Him after His return to earth. We will have kingdom responsibilities at a later time, but beforehand, we will rest, rejoice, and revel at the marriage supper of the Lamb.

Fourth, the God who places "the solitary in families" (Psalm 68:6) will surely give us abundance of time to reunite with loved ones and enjoy new connections with fellow believers. Many saints experience lengthy stretches of loneliness on earth, but they won't feel that heavy burden for even a fleeting moment after they meet Jesus in the air. It will please the Lord to provide fellowship with our families, friends, new acquaintances, saints who lived before us on the earth, and even men and women we read about in Scripture.

And *fifth*, our time in Heaven during the interval between the Rapture and Second Coming will be spent in great merriment as we celebrate our wedding (see chapter 7).

Q. Will we recognize family and friends?

A. Yes, in Heaven we will know family and friends, and they will know us. Just as Jesus' followers recognized Him after He rose from the dead, so our acquaintances from this life will recognize us. Furthermore, not only will our relationships continue, but they will be even better, because they won't suffer any of the consequences that come from human weaknesses or sin.

Since our flesh will no longer hinder the Holy Spirit's work inside us, we won't forget names as we sometimes do now; further, we believe He will enable us to even recognize people we've never met on earth, even those whom we have studied about in Scripture.

Q. How can I be happy in Heaven if someone I loved on earth isn't there?
A. The Bible tells us this in Revelation 21:4:

> And God shall wipe away all tears from their eyes; and there shall be no more death, neither sorrow, nor crying, neither shall there be any more pain: for the former things are passed away.

While some interpret this as occurring only after God creates the New Heavens and New Earth, the eternal state, the fact that Heaven is perfection makes it necessary for this verse to apply to the moment we leave this earth and are at home with our Lord.

From our earth-bound perspective, to lose an unsaved loved one is heart-wrenching. However, in Heaven, we will have the mind of Christ at the moment we are with Him eternally. He tells us He will have to say to the unbeliever, "I never knew you." This is not just a judicial advisory on the part of the Lord. It means He will forget for eternity the individual who has never come to Him.

We certainly can't understand this at present, but when we have the mind of Christ and see Him as He is, we will be like Him. We, too, will have the ability to forget, just as God has that ability. This isn't a pleasant thought right now, but we will understand it all by and by.

Q. What type of body will we have?
A. At the time of the Rapture, whether we are already with the Lord or alive at the time, Jesus will give us immortal, imperishable bodies

(1 Corinthians 15:49–54). Philippians 3:20–21 reveals that they will be like that of our Lord after His resurrection:

> But our citizenship is in heaven, and from it we await a Savior, the Lord Jesus Christ, who will transform our lowly body to be like his glorious body, by the power that enables him even to subject all things to himself.

The passages that describe the Risen Christ's appearance offer many clues about what our bodies might be like. For example, Jesus was able to appear behind locked doors. We aren't sure we will have that capability in eternity, but we will be able to swiftly move throughout the New Jerusalem and New Earth. We believe that, during the Millennium, we will easily move back and forth between our residence above and planet earth.

This is a reality that's often overlooked in churches today, but it's truth that brings great comfort during the perilous days in which we live.

Q. Will we have supernatural powers?
A. The simple answer is yes. We have already expressed our belief that we'll be able to move back and forth between earth and the New Jerusalem during the Millennium. The huge size of the city will not prevent us from being able to instantly visit loved ones who might live hundreds of miles away.

Depending on the roles the Lord assigns us in the Millennium, we will have special powers to accomplish those tasks. With nothing to hinder the work of the Holy Spirit inside us, we will have supernatural insight when it comes to dealing with the inhabitants of the earth during Jesus' reign.

Author Peter Kreeft asserts the likelihood that we will have superior powers in Heaven:

Powers that are now largely denied us, for our own safety, will be restored to us when we have learned to use them well. When our souls follow the will of God like orchestra players follow the baton of their conductor, then we will play in harmony. But just imagine what havoc God would allow if he gave us preternatural powers over nature in our fallen condition![101]

Q. How old will we be?
A. Since aging is a product of the Fall, a curse upon humanity, we will not grow old in eternity. We will have the appearance of youth minus the imperfections we gained from aging. We believe we will have perfect, youthful-looking bodies that those who knew us on the earth will instantly recognize.

Q. Will children arrive in Heaven as young adults?
A. Scripture doesn't answer this question, but we know Jesus loves children, which makes it an argument in favor of them maturing while in the New Jerusalem versus arriving as young adults. Might Jesus allow them to continue growing up in the care of their parents? We don't know. We do know we will forever enjoy relationships with our saved offspring, and those of us who are grandparents can greatly look forward to spending time with our grandkids.

Q. Will we remain married?
A. The Lord, in answering a question about marital relationships in eternity, said the following:

> For in the resurrection they neither marry, nor are given in marriage, but are as the angels of God in heaven. (Matthew 22:30)

Of course, we will know our spouses in eternity and will spend time with them just as we will with all our loved ones, but our relationship with our spouses will not remain the same. We know from Scripture that God places a high value on families, and that will continue in eternity. We will have an abundance of time to spend with them in eternity, as well as many opportunities to form new connections.

Q. Will we be lonely in Heaven?
A. No, we will never again experience the loneliness so many saints endure in this current life. *Never again will we long for interactions with others or meaningful fellowship.*

Walls between us and others that exist in this life will come down as everyone in Heaven remains free from sin. There will be joyous reunions and a constant flow of new relationships that will keep us far away from the pangs of solitude we sometimes feel in this life.

Q. Will we retain our uniqueness as men and women?
A. The most compelling reason for retaining our gender identity is Satan's current all-out attack on it. The cancel culture of our day is doing all it can to destroy our uniqueness as men and women, which is an attack upon God who created us the way we are. We believe people will retain their gender identity, but without the physical intimacy of husbands and wives.

The Lord is the one who created us as males and females, and His purposes for doing so will continue into eternity. According to author Peter Kreeft:

> We will be "like the angels" in "neither marrying nor being given in marriage," according to Christ's answer to the Sadducees (Matt. 22:30), but not in being neutered. Sex is first of all something we are, not something we do.[102]

God designed all of us as unique individuals and our gender is key to His sovereign purposes for us both now and forever. We will retain our God-given uniqueness as males and females in Heaven.

Q. What will we wear?

A. Fashions have not only varied in our lifetimes, but also throughout history and the world as well.

Although the Bible doesn't specifically answer this question, we find some indications of what to expect in the book of Revelation. John described the twenty-four elders, who represent the Church in Heaven after the Rapture, as being "clothed in white garments" (Revelation 4:4). When the apostle saw the Tribulation saints standing before God's throne in their pre-resurrection state, he noted that they were all "clothed in white robes" (Revelation 7:9). At the marriage supper of the Lamb, the Church appeared dressed in "fine linen, bright and pure" (Revelation 19:9, 14).

When we are in the New Jerusalem and with the Lord upon His return, we will wear white, fine linen garments, likely robes, that will portray our purity as redeemed saints. The word for "bright" in Revelation 19:9 denotes clothing that is radiant and glowing in appearance. Will we retain our shining appearance while carrying out our assignments on the earth? Should that be the case, it would definitely set us apart from those who enter the Millennium in their natural bodies.

Q. Will we eat and drink?

A. Yes, Jesus ate after His resurrection and, as we read in Matthew 26:29, He told the disciples the following after instituting the Lord's Supper:

> But I say unto you, I will not drink henceforth of this fruit of the vine, until that day when I drink it new with you in my Father's kingdom.

Not only will we drink in Heaven, but the Lord will do so with us. The Bible also tells us about the previously mentioned marriage supper of the Lamb (Revelation 19:9), which certainly implies that we will enjoy a meal with all the redeemed of the Church Age. The prophetic words of Isaiah 25:6–9 tell of a grand feast the Lord will prepare for "all peoples" at some point in the future.

Randy Alcorn, in his book *Heaven*, wrote:

The best meals you'll ever eat are all still ahead of you on the New Earth.[103]

We won't eat because we need to, but for the enjoyment and the fellowship it will create with fellow saints.

Q. Will we sleep?

A. The Bible doesn't specify whether or not we will sleep in Paradise. Because our bodies will be imperishable, we will not *need* to sleep. With Lord's glory lighting up all of the New Jerusalem and the earth during the eternal state, the pattern of day and night will likely cease after the Millennium.

Author Randy Alcorn believes we will be able to sleep in Heaven if we choose to do so, because it "is one of life's great pleasures."[104] On the other hand, if it's not a necessity, we might never feel the desire to do so.

Q. Will there be music?

A. Absolutely! We can be sure there will be music in Heaven.

The words of Psalm 92:1 encourage us to "sing praises to your name, O Most High." Another psalm tells us to "come into His presence with singing" (Psalm 100:2). Temple worship in the times of the Old Testament days always included singing the psalms. The God who gave music a place in worship then is the same One we praise today. We can be sure there will be an abundance of music both in the New Jerusalem and on the New Earth.

Singing is a way to worship the Lord both privately and corporately.

Many of the hymns written during the past couple of centuries are rich in theology and reinforce biblical truths.

Besides voicing our admiration of God through songs, will we participate in choirs and orchestras and perform concerts? Some believe this will happen—but, again, the Bible is silent on the subject.

Jonathan enjoyed playing the trombone for several decades, particularly when he played in large church orchestras. Playing hymns while he was alone became a time of worship as he meditated on the words as he practiced. Sometimes he wonders if he will have the opportunity to play the trombone again after this life ends!

Q. Will we participate in sports or exercise?
A. Randy Alcorn, in his book *Heaven*, believes the answer to this question is, "Yes." Even in our glorified bodies, he says, we will participate in competitive sports and feel a need to rest after such exertion. There's definitely a pleasurable aspect to taking part in such activities even though our imperishable bodies won't need the exercise.

It seems quite likely that those who survive the Tribulation and enter the Millennium in their natural bodies will revive competitive sporting activities, especially as the population grows. It's probable that we will even watch such events.

However, the Bible is silent on whether such athletic endeavors will happen in the New Jerusalem or on the New Earth; we will need to wait and see.

Q. What language will we speak?
A. One of Jonathan's beloved teachers in seminary, Dr. Richard Rigsby, firmly believed everyone will speak Hebrew in Heaven. Can you guess what subject he taught?

The God who confused the languages at the Tower of Babel is certainly capable of reversing it when we enter eternity. He may instantly give us all the same language once we arrive in glory. It's also possible that, regardless of the language spoken, we will always hear it in our own native tongue and others will hear what we say in a way they understand. Or might Dr. Rigsby be correct in saying we will all speak Hebrew?

We can be sure of this: Language will never be a barrier in Heaven. We will be able to communicate with all the saints of the Church Age, regardless of when or where they lived during their lifetime. This also applies should we strike up a conversation with the Apostle John.

Q. Will there be animals on the earth in eternity?
A. We know there will be animals on the earth during the Millennium and eternal state based on the words of Isaiah 11:6–9. These verses describe vastly different wildlife than we see now, as they will no longer have a predatory nature.

> The wolf also shall dwell with the lamb, and the leopard shall lie down with the kid; and the calf and the young lion and the fatling together; and a little child shall lead them. And the cow and the bear shall feed; their young ones shall lie down together: and the lion shall eat straw like the ox. And the sucking child shall play on the hole of the asp, and the weaned child shall put his hand on the cockatrice' den. They shall not hurt nor destroy in all my holy mountain: for the earth shall be full of the knowledge of the Lord, as the waters cover the sea.

Some believe the context of the above passage is the Millennium, while others believe it refers to the New Earth. But why not both? It seems unlikely that God would include animals in one and not the other. They were a key aspect of His original, pristine creation before sin entered the world, and it's a safe assumption as well for both the millennial world and the eternal state.

The Bible doesn't mention the existence of animals in the New Jerusalem, but the array of them in God's creation now argues for their presence in Heaven. Will we hear birds chirping and watch hummingbirds flit from flower to flower in New Jerusalem? It's highly likely.

Larger creatures such as elephants, bears, giraffes, and hippopotamuses may only inhabit the New Earth, but that's only speculation on our part.

Q. Will we have pets in New Jerusalem?
A. The Bible doesn't say anything regarding this topic or whether the Lord will raise up our beloved pets from this life for us to enjoy. We defer to the words of Joni Eareckson Tada on this matter:

> If God brings our pets back to life, it wouldn't surprise me. It would be just like Him. It would be totally in keeping with His generous character.... Exorbitant. Excessive. Extravagant in grace after grace.[105]

Whatever the case, we will always experience the Father's lavish love and goodness. His desire to bless us will know no limits once we arrive in our forever home.

Q. How will we perceive and experience time?
A. For creatures bound to the dimension of time, it's impossible to imagine living outside of it. There will always be a starting point to our lives. As we saw in chapter 6, the Lord will most likely take us outside of time as He examines each of the large multitude of saints that He will bring to Heaven with the Rapture of the church.

In biblical prophecy, the seven-year Tribulation will begin with the covenant Antichrist makes with Israel (Daniel 9:27). In Revelation 20:1–10, John repeatedly stated that the Millennium will last one thousand years. During all this time, the cycle of day and night will continue. People on the earth will experience the passage of time and we will be aware of it as well.

However, this changes in the eternal state; there, the sun and moon will no longer exist, and the Lord will be the continual light illuminating both the New Jerusalem and New Earth. Will we mark time in eternity? Will we even care? It will be a much different existence; one we won't be able to fully understand until we get there.

Q. Will we have emotions?
A. We must first understand that even negative emotions, by themselves, are not sinful. The Bible portrays God as being angry, and Jesus displayed the same emotion when He chased away the traders in the Temple (John 2:13–17; Matthew 21:12–13).

We also see that Jesus felt sorrow; He wept before raising Lazarus from the dead (John 11:35). Emotions are part of being human, and that won't cease in eternity.

On the other hand, it's clear that we will sense immense joy as well as love for others in Heaven. All the factors that cause strife in our current relationships will cease in eternity.

Psalm 16:11 says that in God's "presence there is fullness of joy." That's the emotion that will characterize our time in the hereafter beginning with the Rapture. We might feel regret and sadness at the judgment seat of Christ as He examines our service for Him. But we will mostly overflow with happiness as we praise our Savior and worship God the Father in the next life.

Q. Does looking forward to Heaven make us "escapists"?
A. Not at all. During the history of Christianity, it's been those who believed in Heaven who have done the most for others. They are, for the most part, the ones who have built hospitals, cared for the sick, and founded the sciences with the purpose of bettering everyone's life on the earth.

The Samaritan's Purse ministry, for example, has a budget of over eight hundred million dollars to provide relief after disasters, pandemics, and other emergencies. Its founder and director, Franklin Graham, also believes in a hereafter and looks forward to the Lord's imminent appearing, just as do the authors of this book.

Author Peter Kreeft, said the following about whether or not focusing on Heaven is escapism:

> I answer the question with another question, from C. S. Lewis: Who talks the most against "escapism"? Jailers. Is it escapist for a baby to wonder about life outside the womb? Is it escapist for someone on a long ocean voyage to wonder about landfall? Is it escapist for the seed to dream of the flower? It is escapist if, and only if, Heaven is a lie. Those who call Heaven "escapism" are presupposing atheism.[106]

Q. How do I get into Heaven?

A. Cartoon images of people coming up to the gate of Heaven seeking entrance into the city are as far from portraying the truth as the east is from the west. Our eternal destiny is set in this life before we die; we won't have the opportunity to plead our case at the "pearly gates" of Heaven.

Jesus said, "I am the door. If anyone enters by me, he will be saved and will go in and out and find pasture" (John 10:9). Those who, in this life, reject His offer of forgiveness and eternal life will have no opportunity to change their mind after death.

Jesus is the only way to eternal life in the city. "I am the way, and the truth, and the life," He said. "No one comes to the Father except through me" (John 14:6). If you have not yet placed your faith in Christ, please do so today, before it's too late. Jesus is the way to eternal life; if you depend on anything else for your entrance into Paradise, you will fall far short.

Yes, people will come to saving faith in the Savior after the Rapture.

However, you have no guarantee of living until that happens or of surviving the chaos that will ensue in the world immediately after the Lord suddenly removes His Church and His wrath begins to fall on the earth's remaining inhabitants.

Q. How should anticipating eternity affect our lives?

A. First of all, thinking about what will happen after death should cause us to consider whether we've placed all our hope for eternity and the forgiveness of sins upon Jesus. All our goodness, morality, and efforts to live good lives will fail unless Christ is our Savior and our hope is in Him alone.

Scripture provides at least four ways our study of the hereafter should affect us.

1. **It should have a purifying influence on our lives** (1 John 3:2–3). The fact that the Rapture can happen at any moment should motivate us all the more to live in a manner pleasing to the Lord. Particularly, all the prophesied signals of Jesus' return converging as never before in history should give us a continual awareness that He might take us home today. How can that not encourage us to live in ways that are more pleasing to God?

2. **Since God will someday destroy everything in this world with fire, it compels us to conduct our lives with "holiness and godliness"** (2 Peter 3:11). Such awareness of the gravity of things to come adds a certain soberness to our lives and an increased awareness of the destruction ahead for this world (1 Thessalonians 5:1–11).

3. **It leads us to embrace the two-world perspective the Apostle Paul described in 2 Corinthians 4:17–18.** Although we can't ignore the temporal things of this life along with our daily responsibilities, our awareness of Bible prophecy urges us to place a higher value on eternal realities (Romans 8:18).

4. **It leads to steadfastness in our service for the Lord.** After writing about the Rapture and our receipt of glorified bodies, Paul offered the following encouragement in 1 Corinthians 15:58:

Therefore, my beloved brothers, be steadfast, immovable, always abounding in the work of the Lord, knowing that in the Lord your labor is not in vain. (ESV)

There's something about being confident about the Lord's soon return that enables us to stand firm in serving Him, knowing that it's from Him we will receive our rewards rather than from those we serve in this earthly life.

HEREAFTER UNVEILED

"There are far, far better things ahead than any we leave behind."

~C. S. LEWIS

The above quote by C. S. Lewis, one of his most popular, encapsulates the theme of our book. What lies ahead for the redeemed in the hereafter is indeed far better than anything on earth. In fact, it's far better than anything we can even imagine.

The personal testimony of one Terry James was briefly offered earlier in this book. However, the experience so profoundly exemplifies this theme that we felt directed to include a more expansive account of his clinical death experience on Good Friday, April 22, 2011.

This is not to aggrandize Terry in any sense whatsoever. And we recognize that many view such experiences with a high degree of skepticism. The testimony is, however, truthful and meant only to glorify God and offer what we believe is a firsthand account of life after the Rapture. Our prayerful hope is that this will comfort those who are born again and will bring those who are not to saving faith in Jesus.

TERRY JAMES' TESTIMONY

So it was that God, my Heavenly Father, has dealt with me through the clinical death I experienced Good Friday, April 22, 2011. I went through that ordeal, and I am here, now, writing about it for purposes He has determined. It is not a coincidence that brings either you or me to this point in the book.

God has shown me, without the slightest doubt in my spirit and mind, exactly what my near-death experiences mean. Therefore, without any reservation, I am putting down for the record the message I know He wants me to deliver.

I write these things with a profound sense of humility, however. I am nobody special, other than a child of God through the shed blood of my Savior and Lord, Jesus Christ. On second thought, I guess that does make me someone special—in God's holy eyes, but only because of what Christ did for me on that old, rugged cross. Like the Apostle Paul framed his own relationship with God, the same applies to my case. Terry James would be the chief among sinners, if not for the righteousness God the Father sees when looking at His Son, Jesus Christ, in evaluating my life now that I am His child.

Believe It or Not

Many who major in teaching and preaching about miracles and wonders use the following Scripture passage to launch into stories of great ecstatic pronouncements:

> And it shall come to pass afterward, that I will pour out my spirit upon all flesh; and your sons and your daughters shall prophesy, your old men shall dream dreams, your young men shall see visions. (Joel 2: 28)

This time spoken of by Joel the prophet has not yet happened. The word for when this era will be reached is the Hebrew *achar*, which means "afterward" in English. This prophecy of miraculous visitations, when old folks will dream dreams and young men and women will see visions, is scheduled for after Israel, God's chosen nation, will as a people recognize that God is their strength and provider. The people of Israel today do not look to the God of Heaven. They haven't received reconciliation through repentance yet. This prophecy is for when King Jesus rules and reigns upon the throne of David atop Mount Zion during the Millennium (Revelation 20:1–5).

The world certainly hasn't reached the Millennium. Jesus is still at the Father's right hand. So, I didn't have a dream or vision because we've reached that spectacular time prophesied for the millennial reign of Christ. However, the Lord can and does reach into any and all ages (dispensations) He desires, and God, the Holy Spirit, it is affirmed in my spirit, did so on April 22, 2011.

I could, in order to sound self-deprecating, tell you the Lord just on-the-spot decided to use my widow-maker heart attack, when it happened in the course of unfolding time in my life, to say through my experience what He wants said. But that isn't what really happened. It was much more specific and preordained than that. God reached down and took my spirit into…where, I'm not certain. But for sure He took me from this earthly dimension and stood me in front of myriad young, beautiful, wildly cheering, jubilant beings. It was no coincidence. It was done for an absolute divine purpose. God chose the likes of me—a physically, totally blind, aging sinner saved by His grace— to go through this extremely brief but spectacular visit to the fringes of Heaven where I could see perfectly well.

Some of what this all means came to me almost immediately, when I was hooked to wires leading to monitors and IV tubes while in the cardiac intensive care unit. Other aspects of what my heart stopping and being instantly in the presence of those heavenly beings is all about were, in some cases, revealed much later, while I was thinking in directions totally unrelated to the experience. I'm convinced it was the voice of the Holy Spirit I heard, almost audibly, on each and every occasion.

Believe me, I am most reluctant to embrace in any sense metaphysical, experiential expressions of the Christian faith. By that, I mean stories of supernatural intervention by God into the lives of believers today through such things as dreams, visions and miraculous healings—like missing limbs replaced, or, well, people being brought back to life after being dead and embalmed.

Do I believe God performs miracles today? Absolutely—every hour of every day. But they are very rare in the truly spectacular sense of performing miracles. For example, I've never heard of a single documented case in modern history in which someone whose arm was totally withered— to the point that it was a useless blob of flesh—was restored to full use like the person's other arm, simply by a faith healer or other person touching it and praying. I've never seen verified accounts of a person born without a leg, foot, or eyes suddenly had those miraculously added to the body through a faith healer's touch.

I'm a believer and trust my Lord implicitly. However, I'm also a rational being who finds it prudent to, when it comes to dealing with human beings, do what President Ronald Reagan said about dealing with the Soviets: "Trust, but verify."

So, with all these things in mind, why should you—or anyone—believe me and my recounting of the wondrous visit to the heavenly dimension on Good Friday of 2011? All I can say is that I know it happened, because I was there among that throng of heavenly beings each time I heard the computer-like blip and my heart stopped. The Lord has told me in the deepest reaches of my spirit to report to you that visit. He has also given me what it means—and in remarkable detail—considering the brevity of the trip to and from that realm.

Believe it or not. Do with it what you will. The following is my faithful execution of the commission the Lord gave me: reporting what my Heaven vision means to this generation.

HeavenVision: The Interpretation

Near the end of the year 2010, two projects came into my thoughts. The first was for our raptureready.com website—a series of articles I soon gave the title "Scanning a Fearful Future." The second project was to author a book on Heaven, which my mother and her sister wanted me to do.

I began writing a series of ten articles for our Nearing Midnight column on the website. The last one appeared on the site on January 24, 2011. Sometime in late December of 2010 or early January 2011, I decided to start the book project. My subsequent notes indicate I named the book *HeavenVision: Glimpses of Glory*. The date in my notes for beginning the book project was February 4, 2011.

I also made a note to consider building the *HeavenVision* book around near-death or clinical-death experiences of individuals—if I could find some that rang true, according to what the Bible has to say about life, death, and Heaven.

One of the primary reasons I wanted to write the "Scanning a Fearful Future" series was to try to help provide answers from the prophetic Word, because so many who visit our raptureready.com website were concerned about where the national and worldwide economic upheaval was leading.

Also, we were getting an increasing number of emails accusing us of being heretics who were leading people to Hell with our pre-Tribulation Rapture teaching. Christians should be prepared to face the coming Tribulation and Antichrist, we were told in the scathing diatribes. By not preparing Christians to face the Beast of Revelation 13, they would not know to reject his mark and number. As a matter of fact, many of the quite excoriating emails stated that we were already in the Tribulation.

While the two projects were going through my mind, I prayed: "Lord, I know what your Word says. The pre-Tribulation view of the Rapture is the correct one, I believe. But, nonetheless, please give me absolute confirmation of this truth. We don't want to lead people astray." I also asked the Lord to give me affirmation in my spirit that what He gave me to write in the "Scanning a Fearful Future" column, I had faithfully written.

These were matters I took constantly before the throne. One other matter was in my thoughts, if not my prayers. It went something like: "Wouldn't it be interesting to have a near-death or clinical death experience, myself? Just die briefly, and have the Lord bring me back in order to tell the story of a spectacular experience that He allowed. That would really give the book credibility!"

The Lord has a sense of humor—I now have no doubt. The old adage, "Be careful what you wish for" definitely applies.

The hospital records show I clinically died not once, but three times on Good Friday, no less. My amazing experience of being in that other place with the cheering young people, then resurrected, in a manner of speaking, was the Lord making a statement, I've been shown.

The first thought to penetrate my realization while I was in the hospital bed was that the throng of cheering young people who greeted me each time my heart stopped was—and is—the cloud of witnesses of Hebrews 12:1–3.

The second thing that pierced my spiritual understanding, several days later, was that the cheers that greeted me in that heavenly setting were the approval of my writing and teaching Bible prophecy. All of this was affirmation from the Heavenly Father—not just for me, but for all of His children who believe and disseminate Bible prophecy in these last of the last days before His Son calls the Church to Himself (Revelation 4:1–2), as He promised in John 14:1–3.

My commission, as seared into my realization, is to pass along that God, through the cloud of witnesses I saw, was giving His nod of approval to His people for getting out His prophetic truth whenever and in whatever way opportunity is presented.

Later, over the weeks and months of recuperation, and to this point, the Lord has given me a deeper understanding of those Good Friday glimpses of glory.

My "Scanning a Fearful Future" articles are key to my vision of Heaven. I prayerfully began writing them in hope of allaying the fears that were arriving fast and furious via email at a time when America and the world's economic collapse looked imminent.

The question in every email on the topic of the "coming economic collapse" was based upon a well-known TV pundit's declaration that Americans could awaken on any morning and find that the world had changed completely. The US dollar would no longer be of any value. A worldwide depression would quickly bring changes that would require martial law and the imprisonment of all who didn't toe the mark of what Big Brother demanded.

The Holy Spirit prompted me to write the series, examining carefully what biblical prophecies for the end of the age had to say about this matter.

Most of the emails expressed a fear that Christians in America would be put in FEMA internment camps—which were said to be proliferating around the country, according to many blogs and conspiracy-theory-laden websites.

Would Christians in America face martyrdom—or maybe even the Antichrist regime? Maybe the pre-Tribulation Rapture view wasn't true after all. Maybe we were already in the Tribulation!

The series covered ten weeks, so there isn't room in this section of the book to include all of those articles. However, the bottom line in answer to the fear-filled emails is the following—the conclusion of the series.

Jesus Provides the Answer

The series of articles brought me, in the final analysis, to the words of the greatest of all prophets: the Lord Jesus Christ:

> And as it was in the days of Noe, so shall it be also in the days of the Son of man. They did eat, they drank, they married wives, they were given in marriage, until the day that Noe entered into the ark, and the flood came, and destroyed them all. Likewise also as it was in the days of Lot; they did eat, they drank, they bought, they sold, they planted, they builded; But the same day that Lot went out of Sodom it rained fire and brimstone from heaven, and destroyed them all. Even thus shall it be in the day when the Son of man is revealed. (Luke 17:26–30)

Another Gospel account expounds further upon Jesus' prophecy:

> But of that day and hour knoweth no man, no, not the angels of heaven, but my Father only. But as the days of Noe were, so shall also the coming of the Son of man be. For as in the days that were before the flood they were eating and drinking, marrying and giving in marriage, until the day that Noe entered into the ark, And knew not until the flood came, and took them all away; so shall also the coming of the Son of man be. Then shall two be in the field; the one shall be taken, and the other left. Two women shall be grinding at the mill; the one shall be taken, and the other left. Watch therefore: for ye know not what hour your Lord doth come. (Matthew 24:36–42)

No catastrophic man-made or natural event will throw the nation and world suddenly into the time of apocalyptic chaos. It will be Christ's sudden call to His Church, the Rapture, that will bring on God's judgment of America as well as the rest of the world.

It will be business as usual, according to Jesus' words, with people buying, selling, building, marrying, etc., right up until the moment born-again believers instantaneously go to be with their Lord.

Jesus couldn't have been prophesying about His Second Advent (Revelation 19:11), because, at that point, the Battle of Armageddon will be raging in the valley of Megiddo, it will not be business as usual, as Jesus indicates in the passages from Luke and Matthew. By that time, as many as two-thirds of humanity will have been killed by the events of the Tribulation.

The Lord of Heaven, Himself, is preventing the total collapse of the world economic system, as He is keeping an all-out war from breaking out in the Middle East.

When Christ steps out on the clouds of glory and shouts: "Come up here!" (Revelation 4: 2), judgment will begin to fall upon America and the world that very day.

Afterthoughts…

Not long after I began writing, *HeavenVision: Glimpses into Glory*, I was totally engrossed in listening to a television program. I don't remember what the program was about; it may have been a ballgame. Out of seemingly nowhere, an inner voice spoke almost audibly.

"Terry, do you remember praying all of those months, before the Good Friday experience, asking for spiritual confirmation that the pre-Tribulation view of the Rapture is the absolute truth from my Word? Well…what do you think that cheering group of youngsters was all about?"

It was all I could do to keep myself from leaping through the ceiling from my sitting position, even without any assistance from the Rapture experience! The epiphany was stunning! I could almost hear the smile of holy amusement in that revelation.

The next moment brought the humbling realization that the Lord of all creation would be so loving as to spend such an intimate moment with someone like me.

I was being applauded for teaching, specifically, the pre-Trib Rapture view. The Lord thus assured me of the true meaning of the Apostle Paul's writing in 1 Corinthians 15:51–55 and in 1 Thessalonians 4:13–18 regarding Jesus' appearing.

Again came the prompting in my spirit that the encouragement wasn't for me alone, but for all who hold to the pre-Trib understanding in these final hours of the age.

A while before that, another epiphany had illuminated my spiritual understanding of my visit to what I believe must have been somewhere near the portals of Heaven. As I was standing before that crowd of enthusiastic young people each time my heart stopped beating, one face stood out from among them. Her smile was wide, her expression beaming, while she was thrusting her arms upward, as if celebrating victory at a sports event. On the third and last visit to that otherworldly place of stunning beauty and absolute peace, she looked over at me while we were all running as if in a race, her hands raised in victory. She was laughing, her beautiful expression bursting with unbridled exultation.

That image was constantly with me for more than a month following my trip to that realm. The identity of the woman emerged suddenly into my mind at a rare moment when I wasn't thinking about my near-death event.

While the last vestiges of my eyesight had been fading to darkness because of the hereditary disease Retinitis pigmentosa, I had begun my first book of Bible prophecy, *Storming toward Armageddon*. During that time, I became friends with an elderly woman who could no longer attend our church because she had reached the advanced stages of osteoporosis.

She was a great Christian who loved Bible prophecy, and who was also a very good poet. Many of her writings involved prophecy from God's Word, as a matter of fact. Additionally, she taught several classes of young women each week during Bible studies in her home.

We talked on the phone regularly, and I visited her from time to time. She was excited that I was about to become the author of a book about prophecy. I asked her if we could use one of her brief poems in that book. She readily agreed, and we put one at the beginning of *Storming toward Armageddon*. We also put her poems in my next two books, and she lived to see them in print.

My friend began to lose her ability to see, so we could commiserate over our mutual eye problems. Her health declined quickly, and she died before she lost her eyesight totally.

The Lord has confirmed in the deepest reaches of my spirit that the dynamic, cheering young woman in my visit to the outskirts of glory, whose beautiful face continues to be etched in my mind's eye, is Arbra Carman—my wonderful friend and Christian sister.

My clinical death and being brought back to write prophecy books in God's service for more than twelve years since was so impressive to the cardiology association of my state in 2011 that they gave me the "Cardiology Patient of the Year" award. They invited me to speak at their convention, which I did soon after my recovery. I was able to thank them for their marvelous medical action on my behalf. More than that, I was given the opportunity to witness to the saving power of the Lord Jesus Christ, who alone holds the keys to life, death, and Hell.

Through that, the Lord allowed me to tell of the hereafter that awaits each and every person who accepts the great grace gift the Heavenly Father offers through the sacrificial death, burial and resurrection of His Beloved Son, Jesus Christ.

Here is the only way to be with Christ forever within that hereafter. We urge you to follow the Lord's invitation:

That if thou shalt confess with thy mouth the Lord Jesus, and shalt believe in thine heart that God hath raised him from the dead, thou shalt be saved. For with the heart man believeth unto righteousness; and with the mouth confession is made unto salvation. (Romans 10:9–10)

THE LAND OF WHAT MIGHT HAVE BEEN

By Jonathan C. Brentner

Note: Jonathan wrote the following many years ago as a way to help him forget about past disappointments in his life and look forward to the joys of eternity.

The past is a lonely place. Most often we journey to this land by ourselves, relive its memories in the solitude of our minds, and linger there, thinking about what might have been.

This "Land of What Might Have Been" bears a striking resemblance to J. M. Barrie's fictional island, "Neverland," where Peter Pan fled to escape reality. Like little boys refusing to become adults, we refuse to let go of dreams that are now only faint memories. We tenaciously hold on to the past, not realizing there is only air in our hands. I know this, because I've been to this deserted isle many times.

Our stay in the Land of What Might Have Been is risky. There, the pirate of our souls attacks us with sharp arrows:

"You fool! You should have known better."

"HA! You got what you deserved."

"You are the guilty one!"

"It's all your fault, you know; you should have seen it coming."

And on it goes in the land of What Might Have Been. No over-grown boy in tights flies to our rescue in this realm. We're there seemingly all alone, feeling the pain, shouldering the burden, and soaking our pillows with tears.

Failed plans, broken relationships, crushed dreams, and telephone conversations with old friends all take us back to this desolate place where, hard as we try, nothing changes.

There is another land, however, called the "Land of What Will Be." It is a joyful place, full of activity and people. Those burdened with the past, however, rarely feel the pleasure of this brighter shore.

Two men, with help, were able to leave the Land of What Might Have Been and experience the joy of the Land of What Will Be.

As we join these men traveling to their home in the early evening, we notice their heads hanging low. With much sadness, they rehearse the events of the past few days. The one who was to save their nation had been killed, put to death on a cross as a common villain.

"If only... If only he had lived. What would it have been like? Freedom from Roman bondage. A safe home for our people. If only he were still alive. Can you imagine how great that would have been?"

As they languish in the Land of What Might Have Been, clinging to faded hopes, a familiar stranger approaches from behind. "What are you guys talking about?" he asks.

"Are you the only one in this country who doesn't know what has happened these past several days, how Jesus of Nazareth was betrayed and put to death?" one of the men replies. "Now, to make matters worse, women have visited his tomb and reported that it is empty. They say an angel told them He is alive. What could have happened to the body?"

Undaunted, the stranger becomes their teacher, explaining the ancient Scriptures to them. "The prophets clearly foretold that the Messiah would have to suffer first, and then enter into His glory," he says. Going on, he begins with Moses, and gives the pair a course on Old

Testament prophecy far surpassing all that anyone had ever heard before or since that time.

As the two approach their home, their hearts are burning with hope. They invite the stranger in for supper; there, as he gives thanks and breaks the bread, they recognize him.

"This is our Master—He is alive! He has risen from the dead! He is here, in our home, eating at our table!"

As soon as these disciples recognize Jesus, He vanishes. Immediately, they get up and race back to Jerusalem, their feet barely touching the ground.

The same Savior who brought hope and joy to those saddened travelers so long ago knows all about our shattered dreams, painful past, crushed hopes, and troubled hearts. He stands with us in our pain and feels all the pangs of our loneliness.

But He also stands at the edge of the Land of What Might Have Been and bids us to leave that barren territory.

It is not a call to fame and fortune, at least not in this life. We may discover that our circumstances do not change. They may even get worse; mine did. The disciples who reveled in the Resurrection that first Sunday would face years of persecution for their faith. Most would be put to death for proclaiming that Jesus had risen.

What, then, is the appeal of the Land of What Will Be?

Hope.

It's not the kind of hope we think of when we express a desire for the weather to be sunny and warm tomorrow when, in fact, it quite possibly might storm or snow all day.

This hope is certain. Our future joy is just as sure as Christ's resurrection, which guarantees it with absolute certainty for all those who know Him as their Savior.

But how does this hope sustain us?

Jesus Himself gave us the best illustration of how it works.

First, consider all He endured: Betrayed by a trusted companion.

Condemned in phony and illegal trials, although He had never done anything wrong His entire life. Denial by a close friend. Beaten, whipped, and mocked by people He had created. Being nailed to a cross, the cruelest form of execution imaginable. Scoffed and ridiculed while gasping for air on a cross full of splinters. And, worst of all, He was separated from His Beloved Father in Heaven.

How did Jesus survive all that? What kept Him from losing His mind? How was He able to forgive and reach out to others in midst of such cruel torture?

Hebrews 12:2 explains how:

> Let us fix our eyes on Jesus, the author and perfecter of our faith, who for the joy set before him endured the cross, scorning its shame, and sat down at the right hand of the throne of God.

Can you imagine a joy so great that it can carry someone through all that torment, grief, and agony? Jesus could.

And the good news is that He's willing to share it with us. Just hours before Judas betrayed Him, Jesus spoke of His Father's house in Heaven (the place of the promise of joy that sustained Him on the cross) and assured His followers He would return to take them to a special place He was preparing for them inside that home.

The glory of this coming gathering in Heaven caused the Apostle Paul to proclaim that the sufferings of this life were really nothing compared to the peace and splendor we will experience in eternity. (If you think Paul had an easy life, read 2 Corinthians 11:23–33.) Jesus revealed to Paul that the pleasures of eternity would make his enormous earthly afflictions seem small in comparison.

Our hope is this: Jesus shed His own blood so we might have eternal life and enjoy bliss far beyond anything we can imagine. And He has risen from the dead to demonstrate that this is no pie-in-the-sky promise. It is real. It is certain. He is coming again to take us home.

Will we return to the Land of What Might Have Been in a vain attempt to recapture failed dreams? Will we put our hope in earthly tomorrows that hold no certain promise except that they themselves might someday become candidates for the desolate Land of What Might Have Been?

Or will we place our trust in the One who has cancelled all the charges against us and guaranteed us a certain and secure future, one that even the worst of circumstances on earth can't destroy? Will we fix our eyes on Heaven and let that gaze be our strength in a troubled world? Will we let Him transform our grief into exultation?

We have a choice. We can remain in the Land of What Might Have Been and let the enemy of our souls ravage us with his relentless charges. Or we can put our lives in the hands of a loving and gracious Savior who longs for us to experience the love, forgiveness, and peace He freely offers to all who trust Him. We can look ahead to the glory He has prepared for us in the Land of What Will Be, the realm of the hereafter.

TWELVE SIGNS THE WORLD IS RUNNING OUT OF NORMAL

Jonathan C. Brentner

Note from the authors: In this book, we have concentrated on what we as believers can expect beginning with the Rapture and extending into eternity. We strove to provide a biblical basis for the extravagant delight that lies in our future and have sought to defend our beliefs so you might be confident of your hope in eternity.

We stayed away from venturing into the reasons we expect Jesus to return for His Church in the near future so as not to distract from our main message of the hope that's set before us in the hereafter. However, we're adding this appendix that Jonathan has written to briefly explain why we believe the Rapture will happen in the very near future.

Many people claim that these days are no different than any other time in history. "Sure, things look bad now," they say, "but that was also the case during World Wars I and II. Things have a way of working out so that things return to some semblance of normalcy sooner or later."

I understand why so many question Jesus' soon return, given that it's been two thousand years since He promised to return for us. In spite of the long wait, however, I'm convinced that Jesus' appearing is imminent because of myriad signs telling us that the Tribulation period is right on our doorstep. I have compiled a list of twelve signals that we are rapidly running out of "normal."

If you're weary of waiting and long for the day when you will meet Jesus in the air, please know He's coming soon! If you doubt the Rapture will happen anytime soon, please review the following and read the supporting links.

1. Israel's Miraculous Rebirth as a Nation

Did you know Isaac Newton said Israel would reappear as a nation again? Based on his in-depth study of the books of Daniel and Revelation, he made that startling prediction more than 250 years before it happened.[107]

Newton correctly recognized that the fulfillment of biblical end-times prophecies requires Israel's existence. He also predicted that Israel would build a third temple once it became a nation.

On May 14, 1948, Israel miraculously became a nation again. The amazing rebirth of Israel fulfilled the words of Isaiah 66:8, which predicted that it would happen in a "day."

Israel's supernatural rebirth makes today different than any time before May 1948. It tells us that we live in the last days of human history as we know it.

2. Third-Temple Fever

At the midpoint of Daniel's seventieth week (the Tribulation), Antichrist will defile what many refer to as the Tribulation temple (Daniel 9:2:7). Jesus referred to this desecration as "the abomination of desolation, spoken of by Daniel the prophet" in Matthew 24:15. Paul further described this action as Antichrist sitting in the temple of God, proclaiming himself to be God (In 2 Thessalonians 2:3–8). The apostle added that the Lord will destroy the desolator at His Second Coming.

Though many say Daniel 9:27 refers to a past event, that's impossible. Although Antiochus Epiphanes defiled the temple long before Jesus' birth, that couldn't be the one referenced, because that was still a future event when Jesus was speaking to His disciples concerning the end times (Matthew 24:15). Titus, a Roman general, destroyed the temple in Jerusalem in AD 70, but since the Second Coming has yet to occur, that also couldn't fulfill the seventieth week of Daniel. Jesus Himself will destroy the defiler of the temple at His return to earth (2 Thessalonians 2:3–8), and that didn't happen to Titus.

If we can trust the words of Scripture, there must be a third temple in Jerusalem by the midpoint of the future seven-year Tribulation. That's when the Bible says Antichrist will desecrate it. Do we see evidence today that this will happen in the near future? Absolutely!

Just ten years ago, very few could have imagined today's passion in Israel for the rebuilding of the temple. Did you catch the jubilant celebration in Jerusalem when the five perfect red heifers arrived from Texas? One perfect red heifer is all that's needed for the purification of the temple, and it's highly likely that one of the five will remain undefiled until the age the Law specifies for its sacrifice.

The Temple Institute in Jerusalem has spent more than thirty years researching and preparing furnishings for the third temple. It is currently training Levites to serve as priests.

The Israeli government is planning the infrastructure for the coming temple, including a train that will run from the Ben Gurion Airport to the Temple Mount, as they expect a great many visitors to visit it. The train will not only carry those who want to see the new temple, but it will also have room for worshipers to transport animals for sacrifices.

3. Riders of Apocalypse Kicking and Ready to Go

Revelation 6:1–8 describes what's commonly referred to as the "four riders of the Apocalypse." They are kicking in their stalls and ready to start their trek across the earth. Since current conditions so closely match what the first three horsemen will bring, many believe they're already out of their stalls wreaking havoc.

The fact that we see these conditions already points to the nearness of the Tribulation. Because what we see doesn't match the death toll from these riders (one-fourth of the world's population, which today would be close to two billion), we believe that all four horses are waiting for the Lord to release them at the start of the Tribulation.

The precursors to these events serve as warnings to the world that the day of the Lord's wrath is very near—yet few are paying attention.

4. Digital Currency

If people can buy and sell goods on a cash basis, it would be impossible for Antichrist to control commerce in the way Revelation 13:16–18 predicts. So the fulfillment of this prophecy requires the elimination of cash, and that is precisely what we see in our world.

In 2022, New York Federal Reserve in the US developed a twelve-week pilot program to evaluate the use of a digital dollar using credit card companies and global banks. This test run of the systems necessary for an electronic currency suggests they are ready for its implementation.

Leo Hohmann, a blogger, author, and investigative reporter, wrote about the coming digital currency:

> I believe the new Central Bank Digital Currency, or CBDCs, will make their debut in 2023. And this digital currency will tie in

directly with the digital health certificates on people's cellphones in what will become a personal dossier on every individual, tracking and monitoring their movements and behaviors. If you disobey the government, if you post "disinformation" on the Internet or refuse to stay "up to date" on your shots, they will simply have the banks shut off your money, or restrict its usage to certain places and for certain products. They could also shut off or restrict your digital money if your carbon footprint exceeds your pre-approved monthly allotment.[108]

The US Federal Reserve has announced began a program called FedNow in July 2023, a cashless and digital currency that will quickly move funds between people, banks, and businesses. This also comes amid an increasing number of bank failures in America that are paving the way for a digital currency.

The normality of using cash for purchases is slipping away and with it any privacy regarding our finances. The digital currency will enable governments to monitor how we spend our money, and soon after that, they will control it. India and China are far along in developing a digital currency.

5. Digital Health Passports

At the November 2022 meeting of G20 nations in Indonesia, leaders of the largest economies in the world agreed to work together to implement a "digital health passport" that will track the vaccine status of every human being on earth, as Hohmann noted in the above quote.

This is a necessity for what Antichrist has planned for the latter half of the Tribulation. Below is the path elite powerbrokers of our world have laid out for the future that is leading the world to the fulfillment of Revelation 13:

1. Eliminate cash through a worldwide digital currency.
2. Combine one's online identity for banking with a digital health passport.
3. Monitor all spending, which the Central Bank Digital Currencies will facilitate.
4. Reward or punish people based on their spending habits.
5. Control all spending.
6. Implement what we refer to as the "mark of the Beast."

6. Mark-of-the-Beast Technology

Artificial intelligence (AI) technology, along with the development of gigantic computer databases, also makes today far different than any other previous time in regard to Jesus' appearing.

Prior to the technical advances of the past dozen years or so, Antichrist would have needed an enormous number of people in every nation on earth to enforce the requirement of his mark for all buying and selling. It would have been impossible.

Now, with recent advances in AI and the 5G global network, the technology exists for one person to control commerce everywhere on the planet. Recent advances in technology make the fulfillment of Revelation 13:16–18 not only possible, but increasingly likely!

7. Transhumanism

How will the coming man of lawlessness exercise the complete control over the earth's population, as we see in Revelation 13 and elsewhere in Scripture? The answer is transhumanism.

Transhumanism is the merging of humans with machines, and it's not only something Antichrist needs to accomplish his agenda, but it's also a high priority of the World Economic Forum (WEF) and all the many nations that are now committed to its Great Reset.

The globalists' development of technology for this dovetails perfectly with the fulfillment of Revelation 13:16–18. This is why President Joe Biden recently signed an executive order requiring compliance with the transhumanism agenda. It's necessary for controlling people in the coming New World Order.

The fast-moving advances in AI, coupled with the push to integrate humans with machines, point the soon arrival of Antichrist, who will use these things to enslave the world under his satanic power.

8. Impending One-World Governance

In the last days, a worldwide government will exist, and for a brief time, Antichrist will rule over it (Daniel 7:23–25; 8:18–26; Revelation 13:1–18).

The UN's Agenda 2030 is all about establishing a global governance by 2030 if not well before. The "Great Reset" of the WEF, also known as "Build Back Better," is the economic companion

The rapidly forming one-world government only remains a secret to those who don't want to believe it's happening. The normalcy of individual sovereign nations is ending.

King Charles III of the United Kingdom is a key player in the push for a world government. He is one of the sponsors of the September 2023 SDGs (Sustainable Development Goals) Summit that sought to accelerate the implementation of the UN's Agenda 2030 and the Great Reset.

The UN described the objectives of its seven-year SDG plan as follows:

> The 2023 SDG Summit will take place on 18–19 September 2023 in New York. It will mark the beginning of a new phase of accelerated progress towards the Sustainable Development Goals with high-level political guidance on transformative and accelerated actions leading up to 2030.

Convened by the President of the General Assembly, the Summit will mark the half-way point to the deadline set for achieving the 2030 Agenda and the Sustainable Development Goals. It will be the centerpiece of the High-level Week of the General Assembly. It will respond to the impact of multiple and interlocking crises facing the world and is expected to reignite a sense of hope, optimism, and enthusiasm for the 2030 Agenda.[109]

9. Worship of Creation Rather than the Creator

In the book of Revelation, we see the presence of a one-world religion under the leadership of the False Prophet.

Do we see the rise of such a unified religion today? Absolutely! The stage is fully prepared.

In November 2022, religious leaders from all over the world reenacted the giving of the Ten Commandments. However, the top ten things on their minds consisted of worshiping nature, preserving their god. Combating climate change has become the religion bringing together many diverse faiths as they worship the creation rather than the Creator.

10. Movement of the North Pole

Since 2001, the earth's magnetic north pole has been moving. An article titled "Earth's Magnetic North Pole Is Shifting Dramatically From A Powerful Tug Of War" on the *Forbes* website discusses how this shift has been speeding up in recent years.[110]

Why is this included on this list? It's because of warnings about what happens when the pole shift reaches forty degrees. That's the point at which the north and south poles will swap places.

What's significant about that?

During the Tribulation period, the world will "wobble" (see Isaiah 24:19–20 and Revelation 6:12–17). It is more than a little intriguing that what many predict will happen at the time of the pole shift matches what these prophetic passages indicate will happen in the future.

As the signs of a disastrous pole shift increase, many wonder why it hasn't already happened. We believe it's the result of the Lord's restraining hand through the Holy Spirit stretching out the time for people to turn to the Savior.

11. Mockery of Jesus' Return

Scoffers will arise in the "last days" who will mock our hope in Jesus' soon return (2 Peter 3:2–4). Jude 17–18 also warns of people who will come in the last days to ridicule our hope.

This time has surely arrived!

It's commonplace today for people to make fun of our hope in Jesus' soon appearing. Sadly, even many believers and church leaders have joined the chorus of naysayers. If anything at all, it's surely a sign that we live in the last days of normalcy for this world.

In the early twentieth century, many church leaders mocked the premillennialists who claimed Israel would again become a nation. No one else believed that would happen, but on May 14, 1948, it did. However, that has not stopped the derision. Many continue to laugh at those who believe the Lord will restore a kingdom to Israel. Little do they know they themselves are fulfilling biblical prophecy.

12. Perilous Times Here Again

We live during a time of perilous times "on steroids." While the nineteen characteristics of end-time people, as outlined by Paul in 2 Timothy 3:1–5, have always been evident in some ways, they now define our world more clearly than at any previous time—just as the apostle said they would.

Like with King Belshazzar of Babylon, the handwriting is on the wall (see Daniel 5). The end will not come as swiftly as it did for this ancient king (the Medes and Persians killed him just hours after Daniel interpreted God's message); the signs, however, reveal that God's judgment will soon fall on this world. After the Rapture of the Church, God's wrath will devastate the world.

The good news is the "new normal" that Jesus is bringing will last forever.

When Jesus returns and reigns over the earth from Jerusalem, we will experience life in a glorious kingdom as we reign with Him for a thousand years. This will be a "new normal" worth celebrating, but the future is even brighter and more marvelous! Revelation 21–22 describes the most blissful set of circumstances imaginable.

Refuse to be satisfied with the fake "new normal" that the world offers us. Once we meet Jesus in the air and return with Him to the glory and the hereafter that awaits, what we see then will make our very best days in this life seem mundane and boring.

DON'T MESS WITH REVELATION

By Jonathan C. Brentner

Because so much of what we know about Heaven comes from the book of Revelation, it's important that we trust what it says. For that reason, we must view it as a book of prophecy, which is what it claims to be. Those who spiritualize its contents or say its words have no relevance for today stand on dangerous ground.

During the past few centuries, Satan has reserved his strongest attacks for the books of Genesis and Revelation. The opening chapters of Genesis not only demonstrate our need of a Savior, but also show us God's sovereignty over His creation. Chapter 3 explains how the devil staked his claim on the earth.

It shouldn't surprise us that the devil hates the last book of the Bible. It displays how the Lord takes back ownership of the world, establishes His rule over the nations, casts our adversary into the Lake of Fire, and establishes an eternal world order that's beyond Satan's ability to influence, since he will be in Hell.

In short, the one who now rules as "the prince of the power of the air" (Ephesians 2:2) doesn't want Christians to know he will soon lose his grip on the nations and face eternal punishment for his deception of all the peoples of the earth.

The book of Revelation begins with these words: "The revelation of Jesus Christ." It is all about Jesus' magnificence and power. *From beginning to end, Revelation glorifies our Lord Jesus Christ; it's all about Him.*

Revelation is more relevant than ever as we watch a great many of its prophecies come into sharper focus. Unfortunately, the numbers of those disputing its message continue to rapidly grow, even in churches that claim to believe in the inerrancy and inspiration of Scripture. Although the signs of the nearing fulfillment of Revelation 6:1–8 multiply by the day, most pastors deny its relevance for today.

Revelation begins with a promise of blessing for those who read it and heed its words:

> Blessed is the one who reads aloud the words of this prophecy, and blessed are those who hear, and who keep what is written in it, for the time is near. (Revelation 1:3).

Of course, all of God's Word enriches our lives as we read and study it; however, the Lord says those who read it will reap a unique spiritual benefit.

JESUS' EXALTATION = OUR VICTORY

The exaltation of Jesus on the pages of Revelation is a key reason for the Lord's assurance of a blessing for those who study it. Below are brief summaries of how the book of Revelation glorifies the Lord, and in so doing, looks forward to the time when we will share in His victory.

1. Jesus as the Head of His Church

Chapters 1–3 of Revelation display the Lord in charge of His people, just as Paul described in Ephesians 1:22–23.

Revelation 3:10–11a contains a promise of the Rapture, through which Jesus will take us out of the world before the wrath of the Day of the Lord descends upon "those that dwell on the earth."

Chapters 4 and 5 exalt the Lamb as the only One worthy to open the seals that bind the title deed to this world. The ensuing seal judgments begin the process of the coming King setting up His kingdom as He wrests the nations out of Satan's hands.

2. Jesus as Judge of the Earth in Preparation for His Kingdom

Revelation chapters 6–18 proclaim the Lord's supreme sovereignty over the kings of the earth, nature, and all the forces that now rebel against Him. He will prove the righteousness of His name as He destroys the kingdom of Antichrist along with its lawlessness, deception, and exceedingly great wickedness and lawlessness. Heaven will roar with praise for the Lord Jesus as He celebrates His marriage to the Church and prepares to return with us to the earth.

The day of the Lord's judgments in Revelation will tear the kingdom of this world away from Satan and usher in the thousand-year reign of Jesus.

3. Jesus Reigning for a Thousand Years and Then Forever

Jesus' ultimate display of glory to the earth happens at His Second Coming. He will then destroy the armies of the world gathered against Jerusalem, lock up Satan, and establish His rule upon the earth (19:11–20:6). After putting down a final rebellion, He will judge the world and forever eliminate death and sin (20:7–15).

Revelation 21–22 describes the glorious eternal state of the New Earth and the New Jerusalem. Jesus last words to us, His Church, are these, "Surely I am coming quickly!"

The exaltation of Jesus finds its fullest expression in all of the events recorded in the book of Revelation. Someday we will fill Heaven with praise for our Redeemer (Revelation 19:1–5). We will return with Him and watch as wrests control of the world away from Satan, sets up His kingdom, and takes His rightful place on the throne of David. Jesus will forever destroy sin and death and usher in a glorious eternity.

A CLEAR WARNING

You've heard the phrase, "Don't mess with Texas!" The consequences of rubbing Texans the wrong way are nothing compared to those that result from hampering the message of Revelation in any way.

No other book in the Bible contains such a dire warning:

I warn everyone who hears the words of the prophecy of this book: if anyone adds to them, God will add to him the plagues described in this book, and if anyone takes away from the words of the book of this prophecy, God will take away his share in the tree of life and in the holy city, which are described in this book. (Revelation 22:18–19, ESV)

These words of caution occur because Revelation:

- Exalts Jesus.
- Describes His final victory over sin, death, and Satan.
- Provides immeasurable comfort to believers with its description of how God will deal with this wicked world and bring in a joyous eternal state, including New Jerusalem.

Those who discredit the message of Revelation tread on dangerous ground. Yet so many scoff at its message to their own peril. Below are key ways many in the Church dilute its hope-filled message for the saints.

1. Allegory

Most people today regard the book of the Revelation as an allegory, or just symbolism, rather than the eyewitness account of what John saw and heard, which it claims to be. They *spiritualize* the words rather than allow them to mean what they say.

The spiritualization of biblical prophecy began long ago as a way to combine pagan Greek philosophy with Christianity, especially that of the pagan philosopher Plato, who believed that only the spiritual realm was good. According to him, the material world was inherently evil.

Augustine, who firmly established allegory as the way to approach unfulfilled biblical prophecy, said the idea of a Millennium "would not be objectionable" if somehow "the nature of the millennial kingdom was a 'spiritual one' rather than a physical one."[111] Augustine thus modified his beliefs regarding Jesus' future thousand-year reign on the earth in order to make them comply with the teachings of Plato.

Augustine's hatred of the Jewish people also factored into his eagerness to dismiss the biblical promises regarding the restoration of a glorious kingdom to Israel.

There are many reasons to reject the allegorical approach to the book of Revelation:

- Revelation repeatedly identifies itself as a book of prophecy (1:3; 22:7, 10, 18–19).
- Those who use symbolism to interpret the book of Revelation do not agree among themselves about what is allegorical and literal or how one should interpret the symbols.
- The spiritualization of the text elevates human wisdom above the inspired text since the interpreter (rather than the words) decides the meaning of a passage.

- John's language negates the allegorical approach to the book of Revelation. The apostle used the word "saw" forty-four times by itself and twelve times with the word "looked." He used the word "heard" thirty times. He was clearly not telling us a story, but rather writing what he both saw and heard.

Spiritualization of the words of Revelation turns Christ's triumphal victory over Satan's world system into something that fails to glorify Him or comfort us in any way.

2. History

Preterists say that John wrote the book of Revelation in AD 65 and that the Lord fulfilled all or most of its prophecies in AD 70.

There are many problems with this heresy, including:

- Church history assigns the time of the writing of Revelation to about AD 95.
- Irenaeus, who grew up in the church at Smyrna in the second century AD, wrote that John authored the book of Revelation at this time. If anyone would know when the book first arrived at the church in Smyrna, it would be someone who grew up in that church and received his training in the faith from Polycarp, whom the Apostle John discipled.
- It's readily apparent that the prophetic events described in Revelation have not yet happened. John describes Jesus' Second Coming as a time when "every eye will see him" (1:7). This was most certainly not a first-century AD event.

Even if John wrote Revelation in AD 65, it's highly doubtful that all seven churches would have received the book, read it aloud in all the house gatherings, and made a copy of it by AD 70. For sure, no other church at the time would have seen its prophecies concerning the Lord's return.

Why would the Lord inspire a book of the Bible that would be out of date before the majority of believers living at the time would have a chance to read it?

The preterist approach glorifies the Church rather than the Savior, because it first makes it a kingdom rather than the Body of Christ, and sees the fulfillment of the prophecies in the book of Revelation as relating to it rather than Jesus.

As with all approaches that strip the book of its prophetic value, the preterists' view glorifies the Church rather than the Lord. I have seen this in many conversations with them as well as many amillennialists.

3. Secret Code for First-Century Believers

Another popular yet errant approach states that John wrote the entire book of Revelation in code for the suffering saints who lived during the first century AD. All the arguments against the errant use of symbolism apply here. John recorded future events as he saw them and wrote down the words spoken to him by the Lord and angels.

REVELATION FILLS US WITH HOPE

Those who dilute the message of the book of Revelation by spiritualizing its words, relegating them to history, or telling us that John wrote with a special code do so at their own peril.

Of course, there are verses in the book of Revelation that we don't fully understand. Still other passages have become clearer to all of us as advances in technology have demonstrated how some prophecies once thought impossible are now possible or likely to happen in the future.

But one thing we know for sure: Revelation fills us with hope for what is to come. It provides all born-again saints with exuberant hope as they contemplate their future in eternity.

And, even more significant, the book exalts Jesus from beginning to end, which is what we will do throughout our joyous hereafter.

Our future is all about Jesus and magnifying His Great Name.

NOTES

1. Dr. David Breese, Christian Destiny, Inc. Ministry, quote from Terry James, *Bringing Back Dave Breese: Part II*, on Rapture Ready Website.

2. From *The Saints Everlasting Rest* by Richard Baxter, from a lengthy appendix section in which John F. MacArthur quotes a part of *The Glory of Heaven* (Wheaton: Crossway Books, 1996), p. 173

3. A catheterization laboratory, commonly referred to as a cath lab, is an examination room in a hospital or clinic with diagnostic imaging equipment used to visualize the arteries of the heart and the chambers of the heart and treat any stenosis or abnormality found.

4. J. I. Packer, *Hot Tub Religion* (Wheaton: Tyndale House, 1987), p. 97.

5. Ibid., p. 98.

6. From *The Saints Everlasting Rest,* in MacArthur, *The Glory of Heaven*, p. 178.

7. Ibid., p. 193.

8. Paul David Tripp, *New Morning Mercies—A Daily Gospel Devotional* (Wheaton, IL: Crossway, 2014), January 3 (no page number).

9. Ed Hindson, *Future Glory* (Eugene, OR: Harvest House, 2021), p. 14.

10. Irenaeus, "Against Heresies," *The Ante-Nicene Fathers,* 10 vols., Vol. 1 (Grand Rapids, MI: Eerdmans, 1979), p. 558.

11. Cyprian, *Treatises of Cyprian,* "On the Mortality," section 25.

12. Grant R. Jeffrey, *Triumphant Return: The Coming Kingdom of God* (Colorado Springs, CO: Waterbrook Press, 2001), pp. 175–176.

13. Jonathan C. Brentner, *The Triumph of the Redeemed* (Crane, MO, Defender Publishing, 2021), pp. 199–200.

14. John Eldredge, *All Things New* (Nashville, TN: Nelson Books, 2017), pp. 93–94.

15. David Jeremiah, *Morning & Evening Devotions* (Nashville, TN: Thomas Nelson, 2011), p. 219

16. As shown in the movie, *Before the Wrath.*

17. Ibid.

18. From "The Rapture and the Jewish on the Wedding," Bridal Covenant website, http://www.bridalcovenant.com/wedding1.html.

19. From the movie, *Before the Wrath.*

20. David Jeremiah, *Morning and Evening Devotions* (Nashville: Thomas Nelson, 2011), p. 39.

21. "Home" written by Scott Cash, Ed Cash, and Chris Tomlin; https://genius.com/Chris-tomlin-home-lyrics.

22. Mark Hitchcock and Jeff Kinley, *Global Reset* (Nashville, TN: W Publishing Group—an imprint of Thomas Nelson, 2022), p. 41.

23. Leo Hohmann, "WEF Globalists Meeting in Davos Next Week Warn of War, Economic Collapse, 'New Virus': Are the Four Horsemen Ready to Ride?" January 13, 2023, https://leohohmann.com/2023/01/13/wef-globalists-meeting-in-davos-next-week-warn-of-war-economic-collapse-new-virus-are-the-four-horsemen-ready-to-ride/.

24. Walter Scott, *Exposition of the Revelation of Jesus Christ* (London: Pickering and Inglis [n.d.), p. 122.

25. J. Dwight Pentecost, *Things to Come* (Grand Rapids: Zondervan, 1958). p. 252.

26. Mark Hitchcock, *Heavenly Rewards* (Eugene, OR: Harvest House, 2019), p. 13.

27. Ibid.

28. Pentecost, p. 223.

29. Hindson, p. 72.

30. John MacArthur, *2 Corinthians, MacArthur New Testament Commentary Series* (Chicago: Moody Press, 2003), p. 176.

31. Pentecost, p. 221.

32. Ibid., p. 225.

33. Hindson, p. 80.

34. David Jeremiah, *The Book of Signs* (Nashville, TN: Thomas Nelson, 2019). pp. 210–11. (Quoted in Hindson, p. 81).

35. Hindson, p. 83.

36. Ibid., p. 84 (quoting Lutzer, *Your Eternal Reward*, electronic version).

37. Hindson, p. 90.

38. John MacArthur, *Revelation 12–22, MacArthur New Testament Commentary Series* (Chicago: Moody, 2000), pp. 203–204.

39. Renald Showers, "The Marriage and Marriage Supper of the Lamb Revelation 19:7–9," Israel My Glory Website, June/July 1994, https://israelmyglory.org/article/the-marriage-and-marriage-supper-of-the-lamb-revelation-197-9/.

40. Grant Phillips, "Are You Looking for Christ's Return?" www.raptureready.com

41. Charles Spurgeon, *The Marriage Supper of the Lamb*, August 21, 1887, The Spurgeon Center Website, https://www.spurgeon.org/resource-library/sermons/the-marriage-supper-of-the-lamb/#flipbook/.

42. Ray C. Stedman, *What on Earth Is Happening?* (Grand Rapids: Discovery House, 2003), p. 120.

43. Robert J. Morgan, *Then Sings My Soul, Book 2* (Nashville: Thomas Nelson, 2004), p. 25.

44. Hindson, pp. 113–114.

45. Thomas Boston, *The Kingdom of Heaven*, quoted in appendix 2 of John F. MacArthur, *The Glory of Heaven* (Wheaton: Crossway Books, 1996), pp. 199, 201.

46. Jeffrey, p. 228.

47. Brentner, p. 216.

48. Alva J. McClain, *The Greatness of the Kingdom* (Winona Lake, IN: BMH Books, 1974), p. 433.

49. Jeffrey, p. 116.

50. Ibid., 124.

51. Justin Martyr, "Dialogue with Trypho," *The Ante-Nicene Fathers,* 10 vols., Vol. 1 (Grand Rapids, MI: Eerdmans, 1979), pp. 239–40.

52. Irenaeus, p. 560.

53. Jeffrey, p. 126.

54. Hindson, p. 125.

55. Arnold G. Fruchtenbaum, *The Footsteps of the Messiah*, Third Edition (San Antonio: Ariel Ministries, 2020), pp. 369–370.

56. Brentner, p. 52.

57. Fruchtenbaum, pp. 430–431.

58. Ron Rhodes, *The End Times in Chronological Order* (Eugene, OR: Harvest House, 2012), pp. 192–193.

59. Hindson, p. 139.

60. Ibid.

61. Words by W. C. Martin, "Still Sweeter Every Day.

62. Fruchtenbaum, p. 387.

63. Hindson, p. 132.

64. Pentecost, pp. 538–39.

65. Hindson, p. 145.

66. John MacArthur, Revelation 12–22, p. 228.

67. Ron Rhodes, *Bible Prophecy Answer Book* (Eugene, OR, Harvest House, 2017), p. 195.

68. George N. H. Peters, *The Theocratic Kingdom*, Vol. III (Grand Rapids: Kregel, 1952), p. 465.

69. Ibid.

70. D. Matthew Allen, "Theology Adrift: The Early Church Fathers and Their Views of Eschatology," Bible.org website, chapter 5.

71. Ibid.

72. Pentecost, p. 494.

73. Fruchtenbaum, pp. 470–71.

74. David R. Reagan, *The 9 Wars of the End Times* (McKinney, TX: Lamb and Lion Ministries, 2023), p. 131.

75. Brentner, p. 57.

76. Mark Hitchcock, *The End* (Carol Stream, IL: Tyndale House, 2012), pp. 192–93.

77. David Reagan, "Accident of History?: Why Do So Many Mainstream Denominations Get This Wrong?" Harbingers Daily website, https://harbingersdaily.com/accident-of-history-why-do-so-many-mainstream-denominations-get-this-wrong/.

78. Erich Sauer, *The Triumph of the Crucified* (Grand Rapids: Eerdmans, 1951). p. 152

79. Ibid.

80. Reagan, *The 9 Wars of the End Times*, p. 136.

81. John F. MacArthur, *The Glory of Heaven* (Wheaton, IL: Crossway, 1996), p. 95

82. John Eldredge, *Desire* (Nashville, TN: Thomas Nelson, 2007), p.110.

83. Ibid., pp. 110–111.

84. J .C. Ryle, "Home at Last," sermon in MacArthur, *The Glory of Heaven*, p. 259.

85. Eldredge, p. 119.

86. John Walvoord, *Major Bible Prophecies* (Grand Rapids, MI: Zondervan, 1991), pp. 413–14.

87. Alcorn, *Heaven*, p. 253.

88. Ibid.

89. Wikipedia, "Shangri-La."

90. Alcorn, pp. 172–175.

91. Hindson, pp. 183–184.

92. Hindson, p. 165.

93. Henry M. Morris, *The Revelation Record* (Wheaton, IL: Tyndale,

1983), p. 450, as quoted in MacArthur, *New Testament Commentary*, Revelation 12–22, p. 281.

94. Ibid., p. 451; MacArthur, p. 282.

95. MacArthur, p. 281.

96. Hindson, p. 165.

97. MacArthur, Revelation 12–22, p. 287.

98. Alcorn, p. 410.

99. Hindson, p. 125.

100. Alcorn, p. 410.

101. Peter Kreeft, "What Will Heaven Be Like?" January 28, 2009, Christianity Today website, https://www.christianitytoday.com/ biblestudies/articles/theology/what-will-heaven-be-like.html

102. Ibid.

103. Alcorn, p. 309.

104. Ibid., p. 330.

105. Joni Eareckson Tada, *Holiness in Hidden Places* (Nashville: J. Countryman, 1999), p. 133 (quoted in Alcorn, *Heaven*, p. 401).

106. Kreeft.

107. Stephen D. Snobele, "Statement on the Date 2060," March 2003; updated May 2003 and June 2003. Taken from Isaac Newton Theology, Prophecy, Science and Religion website.

108. Leo Hohmann, "Health Minister Tells G20 Nations They Must Implement WHO-approved 'Digital Health Certificates' Tracking All Human Movement for 'Next Pandemic'," November 15, 2022, https:// leohohmann.com/2022/11/15/health-minister-tells-g20-nations-they- must-implement-who-approved-digital-health-certificates-tracking-all- human-movement-for-next-pandemic/.

109. Un SDG Website: https://www.un.org/en/conferences/ SDGSummit2023.

110. My recent information on this comes from the Facebook page of John Traczyk. He appears to be quite credible and his information is backed up by experts. I am still learning about this, but it very much

seems to be such a sign of the nearing Tribulation that I could not leave it out of this list.

111. D. Matthew Allen, "Theology Adrift: The Early Church Fathers and Their Views of Eschatology," Bible.org, chapter 5.

USE THE QR-CODE BELOW TO ACCESS MANY SPECIAL
DEALS AND PROMOTIONS ON BOOKS
AND FILMS FEATURING DISCOVERY,
PROPHECY, AND THE SUPERNATURAL!

Made in the USA
Coppell, TX
03 January 2025

43891439R00154